Teachers Doing Research

An Introductory Guidebook

R. Murray Thomas
University of California
Santa Barbara

D1113534

PEARSON

Boston   New York   San Francisco
Mexico City   Montreal   Toronto   London   Madrid   Munich   Paris
Hong Kong   Singapore   Tokyo   Cape Town   Sydney

Series Editor: Arnis Burvikovs   **Production Administrator:** Janet Domingo
Editorial Assistant: Kelly Hopkins   **Manufacturing Buyer:** Andrew Turso
Marketing Manager: Tara Whorf   **Cover Coordinator:** Kristina Mose-Libon

For related titles and support materials, visit our online catalog at www.ablongman.com.

Between the time Website information is gathered and then published, it is not unusual for some sites to have closed. Also, the transcription of URLs can result in unintended typographical errors. The publisher would appreciate notification where these errors occur so that they may be corrected in subsequent editions.

Library of Congress Cataloging-in-Publication Data

Thomas, R. Murray (Robert Murray), 1921–
   Teachers doing research : an introductory guidebook / R. Murray Thomas.
     p. cm.
   Includes bibliographical references and index.
   ISBN 0-205-43536-X (pbk.)
    1. Education—Research—Handbooks, manuals, etc. I. Title.

LB1028.T448 2005
370'.72—dc22

2004056056

Printed in the United States of America

10 9 8 7 6 5 4 3 2   09 08 07 06 05

Contents

Preface

Observant teachers, from their daily experiences in the classroom, compile a wealth of educational problems to solve, topics to investigate, and issues to ponder. From those experiences, they also gain valuable insights into potential solutions to those problems, various methods of investigating topics, and ways to settle issues. Some teachers are not satisfied to contemplate such matters in a casual, cursory fashion. Instead, they yearn to investigate issues in a systematic manner that qualifies them to share the outcomes of their study with others—with fellow teachers, administrators, readers of professional books, educators who subscribe to professional journals, and the general public.

In effect, some teachers wish to "do research" on significant educational matters and to disseminate the outcomes of their investigations to broader audiences. However, they often feel poorly prepared to tackle the task. And that's where this book comes in. Its aim is to introduce preservice and inservice teachers to efficient ways of carrying out research that furnishes persuasive answers to educational questions. In pursuit of that aim, the book:

- Traces typical steps in the conduct of research on schooling topics, with each step accompanied by a host of specific examples of what the step entails in the study of a wide variety of questions about life in elementary and secondary schools.
- Describes diverse data-collection methods—both quantitative and qualitative—and identifies the sorts of research questions that each method is well suited to answer.
- Includes practice exercises at the end of most chapters, so readers gain experience applying chapters' contents to life-like research projects.

1

What This Book Is About

This opening chapter offers answers to six questions so that readers will understand at the outset what the book is all about.

- What is research?
- What are schooling topics?
- Why do teachers do research?
- How is information collected?
- Where is such research reported?
- How might this book help?

What is Research?

The term *research* is used throughout this book in a very broad sense to mean "systematically gathering and analyzing evidence appropriate for solving a problem or answering a question whose answer has not been available." Under such a definition, each of the following activities qualifies as *research*, with the purpose of an activity reflected in the question that the research is designed to answer.

- *Question 1.* Which of two ways of teaching the nature of the solar system to third-graders is the more effective?

  The activity. Have two third-grade teachers use Method A for teaching about the solar system and another two teachers use Method B for the same purpose. Then evaluate children's understanding of the solar system in order to determine if one method generally results in a better understanding than does the other method.

- *Question 2.* For advising students about the classes they should take in high school, in what ways are the student admission requirements alike and different among colleges and universities in the state?
- *The activity.* Conduct a content analysis of admission requirements published in the catalogs of the state's colleges and universities.

1

). What are the most common types of difficulties that arise be-
ssroom teachers and the principals of their schools, and what
.... are most often used to resolve such problems?

The activity. Interview classroom teachers and the principals of the
schools in which they teach.

In contrast, the following questions and activities can qualify as *learn-ing* or *searching* but not as *research,* because the answers are already available. The learner's or searcher's task is merely that of finding where the answers are. The task does not involve collecting information and analyzing it to produce a new answer or a new solution.

- *Question 1.* What is the distance from the Earth to the Sun?
  The activity. Hunt under the topic *Solar System* in an encyclopedia.

- *Question 2.* What are the requirements an applicant must fulfill to enroll as a student in the state university?
  The activity. Read the university's catalog or go to the university's website on the Internet.

- *Question 3.* Who is principal of Jefferson High School?
  The activity. Find the school's phone number in the city telephone book, then phone the school and ask for the name of the principal.

What Are Schooling Topics?

For the purposes of this book, a *schooling topic* is "any question generated from events within the classroom or from events outside the classroom that relate to what is taught, to whom, by whom, by what means, and with what result." To illustrate, from within the classroom, the matter of how best to help hard-of-hearing pupils understand what their classmates say during small-group discussions is a schooling topic. From outside the classroom, how the state legislature's mandated achievement-testing program influences the amount of time teachers spend on different subject-matter fields also qualifies as a schooling topic.

Why Do Teachers Do Research?

Teachers' motives in conducting classroom research appear to include one or more of these aims: (a) increase their own understanding, (b) solve classroom problems, (c) contribute to the world's fund of knowledge, (d) further social progress, and (d) promote their own welfare.

Increase one's own understanding

The goal of *increasing one's own understanding* is reflected in the question "Exactly what is the nature of this situation?" That question is often accompanied by "And why are things the way they are?" The first of these questions calls for a factual description of existing conditions. The second involves estimating the causes of those conditions, that is, estimating the *why* behind the conditions.

Here are four topics teachers could study for the purpose of increasing their understanding, with each topic cast in the form of one or more research questions to be answered. The first pair asks only for a factual description of conditions. The second pair asks also for estimates of causes.

- What sorts of difficulties with peer social-relations are common among students who display symptoms of ADDH (attention-deficit disorder with hyperactivity)?
- Which of my fourth-grade pupils' families speak a language other than English in their homes? What are those languages? How much of the time is a foreign language spoken in the home compared to the amount of time English is spoken?
- How many students in my high-school physical-education classes smoke cigarettes or marijuana and how often? When, how, and why did they start smoking? Have they ever tried to quit? If so, with what success? Why have some students been more successful in quitting than have others?
- In what ways do first-graders' ability to concentrate on learning tasks change during the school day? What appear to be the causes of such changes? In what ways, and to what degree, does concentration on learning tasks vary from one child to another, and why?

The immediate intent of each of these projects is only to satisfy the researcher's curiosity without suggesting how the results of the research would — or should — lead to any action on the part of the teacher or the school. However, once the results of such projects are in hand, a decision might be made about what actions, if any, are warranted.

Solve classroom problems

Some topics derive from schooling problems that research might help teachers solve. The goal of such studies is to answer the question "Which solution for the problem is most acceptable?" Thus, the aim is to guide decision-makers in judging how to cope with difficulties encountered in teaching. Studies carried out for this purpose are often termed *action research*, because such projects are expected to provide answers for the problems that initiated the research.

- Which of three math textbooks is best understood by most students?
- What method of teaching computer-literacy skills is most suitable for my sixth-grade class?
- How can I help high school students who are chronic procrastinators learn to start and finish their homework assignments early enough so that the quality of the completed assignments is a valid reflection of their ability?
- What different team-teaching arrangements are best suited to the varied personalities and talents of the teachers in our middle school?

Contribute to the world's knowledge

The aim of a research project can also be to furnish information to other people who are interested in a given issue. In effect, the researcher wishes to know "Who might profit from the results of my project, and how can I best furnish them the results?" For example, many educators would probably like to know the answers to such queries as the following.

- In what ways have the individual-ability differences among high-school students been accommodated in classrooms over the past few decades? What are the advantages and disadvantages of each of these ways?
- What methods have been used by classroom teachers to promote amicable relations among elementary-school pupils who are of different ethnic and religious backgrounds?   How well have such methods succeeded under various classroom conditions and among pupils who exhibit various combinations of ethnic and religious affiliation?
- In different high schools, what behavior in classrooms has been identified as constituting *sexual harassment,* and what sanctions have been applied to teachers or students who have been judged guilty of harassment?
- When parents seek to enroll a child in kindergarten, what criteria do school districts use for determining whether a child will be accepted as a kindergarten pupil? On what line of reasoning do school districts base each of their admission standards?

Further social progress

Sometimes a teacher's chief motive in conducting research is to improve society by correcting social wrongs. Such has been the case with many of the research efforts carried out in recent decades under the banner of postmodernism. Here are four examples.

- Which methods that teachers use in working with immigrant families are the most successful for raising the reading-test scores of children from those families?

- What ethnic stereotypes do teachers hold that affect their views of students' abilities, how valid are those stereotypes, and what steps can be taken to dispel invalid stereotypes?
- What criteria are most suitable for deciding whether a "slow-learning" eight-year-old is better off in a regular classroom than in a special class for slow learners?
- What kinds of behavior of high school students properly qualifies as *bullying,* and what methods are most effective for quelling bullying?

Promote one's own welfare

A strong motive for doing classroom research can also be teachers' viewing research as an important device for furthering their own well-being. The benefit that teachers expect to derive may be of several kinds — satisfy their curiosity about a puzzling question, increase their skills and knowledge, win the admiration of friends and colleagues, impress their employers, and enjoy seeing their work published.

How Is Information Collected?

As soon as a researcher has chosen a question to answer, the next major tasks are those of (a) identifying the kind of information needed for answering the question and (b) selecting an efficient way to collect the information. To gain an initial impression of the range of methods that may be used for collecting data, consider the following samples of available types.

- *Opinion survey.* In a high school's five sections of the required American history course, the teacher assigned each student to identify which six United States presidents were the most influential in the country's history and to explain the reasons for their choices.
- *Activity survey.* A teacher administered a questionnaire to sixth-graders, ninth-graders, and twelfth-graders, asking the students to tell the amount of time they spent on each type of listed activity during a typical day outside of school hours (such activities as watching television, doing homework, doing household chores, engaging in sports, playing computer games, "hanging out" with friends, searching the World Wide Web, engaging in Internet correspondence via e-mail and chat groups, and more).
- *Occupational biography.* After 42 years as a faculty member of a high school English department, a much beloved instructor became the subject of a biography written by a colleague and titled *What It Takes to Inspire.* The biographer attempted to explain why the retiree had produced so many students who had won literary prizes and had become productive authors in later life.

- *Ethnographic study.* The principal of a high school permitted a university graduate student to attend high school classes for one semester in order to conduct a study of the functions of teenage cliques and gangs from the perspective of an insider.
- *Experiment.* A junior-high-school teacher, while pursuing a master's degree part-time in a nearby university, used her four junior-high social-studies classes in an experiment to answer this question: Are students' attitudes toward classroom discipline techniques different if (a) discipline rules and sanctions are imposed by the teacher than if (b) students participate in setting the rules and sanctions? The teacher imposed the rules in two of her classes but engaged the students in helping set the rules in the other two classes, then administered a questionnaire to learn whether students' attitudes toward discipline regulations differed from one pair of classes to the other.
- *Content analysis.* A third-grade teacher analyzed the contents of four primary-grade reading series to identify the moral values reflected in the stories.
- *Historical study.* A special-education teacher searched the archives of a school district's regulations and curriculum plans to answer the question: How have the techniques of teaching intellectually disadvantaged pupils evolved in this school district over the past century?
- *Content analysis plus interview survey.* A teacher who chaired a high-school's curriculum committee wanted to learn how the amount of time required for a curriculum directive issued by a policy-making agency to be implemented in classrooms. He first conducted a content analysis of past directives issued by the federal government, the state department of education, the local school board, the school-district headquarters, and a school's principal or curriculum committee. Then he interviewed fellow teachers to learn if, when, and in what form they had introduced the required curriculum changes in their classrooms.

Numerous additional research methods are described in detail in Chapters 4, 5, and 6.

Where Is Such Research Reported?

In deciding the form in which to report the results of a research project, an author can usefully consider such matters as (a) the range of potential outlets for such reports, (b) what each outlet requires, (c) the type and size of the audience that would likely be interested in the author's product, and (c) how soon the report would become available to that audience.

The variety of potential forms in which research results may be disseminated is great, indeed. Depending on the magnitude and subject-matter of a project, the study's outcomes may be issued as:

A teacher's oral presentation at a faculty meeting
An article in a school newspaper
An item in a newsletter distributed to members of an education association
A bulletin issued by a school district or a university research bureau
A teacher's master's-degree thesis or doctoral dissertation
A paper delivered at an educational conference
A report at a university seminar
An item in a daily newspaper or weekly news magazine
An item on a radio or television news hour
An article in a professional journal
An entry on an Internet website
A chapter in a book
An entire book

Later, in Chapter 9, a detailed analysis is offered about what to consider when choosing the medium through which to issue a research report.

How Might This Book Help?

The process of conducting research on classroom issues can be represented as a series of five major steps or stages: (1) finding and defining a research question, (2) collecting the information needed for answering the question, (3) organizing the information, (4) interpreting the results, and (5) reporting the outcomes.

This book is designed to help researchers by (a) describing the purpose of each stage, (b) proposing alternatives available for performing the tasks under each stage, and (c) suggesting criteria to apply when choosing among the alternatives. Most chapters close with a series of exercises that offer readers an opportunity to apply their understanding of chapter contents to life-like research problems.

2

Finding and Defining Research Topics

The first step in the research process is usually that of identifying a suitable research topic and defining it precisely. Chapter 2 describes ways of performing this step by illustrating (a) useful sources of topics, (b) criteria to apply in distinguishing between better and worse topics, and (c) methods of stating a topic so that the statement fosters the efficient conduct of the research. The chapter also proposes that, early in the research process, it is useful to begin writing the opening portion of the final report.

Sources of Research Topics

As implied in Chapter 1, ideas for research projects can come from both inside and outside the classroom.

Sources inside the classroom

Inside sources can include problems the teacher and students face, potential improvements that can be attempted in the learning program, and decisions to be made.

Problems faced. Here are examples of classroom problems that may become the focus of research. The description of each problem is followed by the question—or questions—that the research is designed to answer.

- *The problem.* In all five of the city's high schools, an increasing number of students have come to school under the influence of illicit drugs or alcohol.

  The questions. What is the incidence of drug and alcohol use among the city's high-school students, how many students come to school under the influence of drugs or alcohol, and what steps can the school attempt to reduce such drug and alcohol use?

9

- *The problem.* Many of Lincoln Junior High School's students—and particularly boys—say they hate poetry, or else they display their disdain for poetry by their obvious lack of enthusiasm when assigned to read or listen to poems.

  The questions. Why do some students dislike poetry, and what methods could be used to change that dislike?

Potential improvements. Apparently, teachers rarely believe that their instructional methods are perfect, so they are often on the lookout for ways to improve the effectiveness of their efforts. This endeavor may lead them to conduct research that assesses the desirability of adopting some new teaching technique. The worth of an innovative method is usually judged in terms of how efficiently it fosters students' mastery of specific learning objectives that may or may not be new objectives for the class. In the following example, the teacher had already subscribed to the general aim of "students abide by the law," but the specific objectives under this general aim were new for the class.

- *The potential improvement.* While reading a past issue of the *Instructor* magazine, a sixth-grade teacher was intrigued by an article titled "Get Kids Interested in the Law." The article described a 150-page book, *CASES—A Resource Guide for Teaching about the Law* (Thomas & Murray, 1982) that used case studies of juvenile crime to teach upper-elementary and junior-high students (a) the nature of laws that juveniles often break (theft, vandalism, glue sniffing, drug use, curfew violation, disorderly conduct, trespassing, and more), (b) police officers' options when they apprehend juvenile law-breakers, (c) juveniles' rights and responsibilities, (d) judges' options when they are imposing sentences, and (e) the nature of life in juvenile-detention facilities. The teacher purchased a copy of the book to try it out with her class. As a way of judging the value of the learning activities recommended in the book, she gave the students a pretest (focusing on the book's specific objectives) before the two-week tryout during which she taught from a different set of cases each day. At the end of the two weeks, she gave a posttest focusing on the same objectives as the pretest but with different specific test items. She then judged the value of the book's activities by the extent of students' improvement between the pretest and posttest.

Choices among alternatives. Teachers are often faced with the task of deciding which of several instructional procedures or ways of treating students will be the most successful. Research can sometimes furnish the guidance needed for making such decisions.

- While attending an inservice program aimed at improving schools' instructional programs, a teacher in charge of a middle school's four sections of eighth-grade mathematics was intrigued by an invited speaker's description of a no-homework approach to teaching mathematics. According to the speaker, students succeed better if their class period is divided into two segments—a *presentation* segment and a *practice* segment—and they are not assigned homework. He said that in a typical 45-or-50-minute mathematics class, the period consists chiefly of the teacher describing a math function and illustrating its use by working out problems on the chalkboard, giving students a few problems to try, and answering their questions. Then homework is assigned, requiring students to apply the function that had been described in class. In the speaker's opinion, students' attention flags after 20 or 25 minutes of a teacher's lecture/demonstration, so that the latter half of the class period is wasted. To prevent this loss of attention, the teacher can assign students problems to solve during the last half of the period. Such an approach, according to the speaker, results in more efficient learning than does the traditional method, and it frees students from homework.

The math teacher decided to test the validity of the speaker's claim by conducting a month-long tryout in which two of his math classes would be taught by his traditional approach (including homework three nights a week) and the other two by the no-homework method. During the month, students in all four sections would study the same topics. Then, at month's end, all would take the same test that assessed their mastery of the month's learning objectives. On the basis of the test results, the teacher would decide which of the two methods—or some combination of them—he would use throughout the rest of the school year.

- In a suburban high school, the instructor of a class titled *Problems of Modern Life* reviewed three textbooks for her class in order to find one she considered gender-fair. By *gender-fair*, she meant books in which neither males nor females were generally (a) stereotyped as having particular personality characteristics that were regarded as typical of their sex (sensitive, logical, intelligent, sympathetic, and such), (b) viewed as properly limited to particular occupations, or (c) blamed for being a bad parent, a bad spouse, or the cause of family separation and divorce. The modern-life problems treated in one textbook were very similar to those treated in another, so the teacher intended to base her choice of a textbook on her gender-fair criteria.

  Her method of investigation involved content analysis. While reading a book, each time she came across a phrase that she judged was an instance of gender bias (either pro or con), she wrote a tally mark beside a gender-bias category. Category titles included *occupation, aptitude or intelligence, family role, assertiveness/submissiveness, initiative, leadership/followership, empathetic/insensitive, seductive, drug abuser, alcoholic,* and others. The textbook that had the fewest number of gender-bias tallies would be the one she planned to adopt for her class.

Sources outside the classroom

Outside stimulants to research can include environmental influences and mandated change.

Environmental influences. The word *environment*, as intended here, refers to physical and social conditions outside the classroom that affect the learning that goes on inside the classroom.

- What do students at Westview Middle School typically eat for breakfast, and how do such diets compare with the diets recommended by nutritionists as being important for maintaining good health and a high level of energy?

- How have the high school's vocational-education classes been influenced by the closure of the city's major furniture-manufacturing company and by the relocation of the region's auto-assembly plant?

Mandated change. Teachers and students are continually subject to new laws and regulations issued by outside agencies and individuals—the federal government, state government, city government, a school district's board of education, trustees of a private school, the superintendent of schools, a faculty committee, a school principal, and more. Such required changes can serve as the stimuli for launching research.

- How has the music instruction received by the city's elementary-school pupils been affected by the board of education's directive to eliminate music teachers from schools as a cost-reduction measure?

- How have the methods of teaching reading in the primary grades (1-3) been influenced by the state department of education recommending the adoption of the *Great Tales Reading Series*?

- How effectively has the high school faculty's stricter student-conduct code reduced the incidence of students' absence, tardiness, and neglect of homework assignments?

Distinguishing Between Better and Worse Topics

To save time and energy—and to avoid undue frustration—persons planning research can profit from testing potential topics against criteria used for distinguishing good topics from poor topics. This task requires not only a clear statement of the topic but also a vision of how the research could be carried out. Specifically, in judging a topic's worth, we need to estimate what information will be needed to answer the research questions, how that information can be gathered, and how it can be interpreted. With this estimate in hand, we can assess a topic's suitability by applying selection-criteria to the plan. Four selection-criteria that I find useful are *novelty, persuasive outcome, cost/benefit ratio,* and *feasibility.*

Novelty. A topic should offer something new, not merely repeat what has already been done.

There are many sorts of novelty that can distinguish a new research project from those of the past. A study can be unusual in (a) the question it is designed to answer, (b) its method of data collection, (c) the people who are studied, (d) its manner of classifying information, (e) the theory on which it's founded, (f) the interpretation of the results, or (g) the way of reporting the outcomes.

Research often takes the form of a *replication study* whose novelty comes from altering some feature of a previous investigation. For example, a first-grade teacher in a rural community reads the report of a study of what children believe—at the time they first enter school—about plant-life reproduction. The reported study had been conducted with first-graders in a large city school. The rural-school teacher may now replicate that study with her own pupils, with the novelty of the replication deriving from the contrast between the rural and urban children's environments.

Persuasive outcome. A study meets the persuasive-outcome standard when the results provide a convincing answer to the research question. Consider the following contrast between two research plans, one whose results would likely be persuasive and another whose results would likely be unconvincing.

- *A persuasive outcome*

   The question. What is the frequency of different kinds of written-composition errors committed by pupils in grades 3, 6, 9, and 12 in the Metro City public schools?

   The researcher. A middle-school English teacher in the Metro City School District.

   The data-gathering method. Teachers at the four grade levels give their students the following assignment.

   "These four large posters you see in front of the room are like a cartoon strip in the newspaper, showing four things that happened when this boy and girl went to a circus. Let's supposed you are writing a letter to a friend, and you want to tell what happened in these four scenes. On the tablet paper that you have on your desk, write that letter to your friend. Tell exactly what you see in the four scenes."

   The researcher then collects the letters written by the students, analyzes the letters for errors, and classifies the results in terms of the number of errors of each type at each grade level.

   The research results. On the assumption that the researcher has done the analysis accurately, most people would likely conclude that the results represent a persuasive answer to the research question.

- *An unconvincing outcome*

   The question. How would high school students react if a person wielding a gun entered their classroom and began shooting?

   The researcher. A high school American-history teacher.

   The data-gathering method. The teacher presents the following task to the students in her four sections of American history.

   > "Imagine that you are in this class when a classmate, who did not attend class this day, suddenly bursts into the room, points a pistol at the students, and starts shooting.
   >
   > "Now, on the sheet of paper that I handed you, write what you would do when the classmate began shooting."

   The research results. It seems unlikely that any thoughtful person would be convinced that data gathered in such a manner answered the research question adequately, because what the students might write could be very different from the way they would behave in an actual crisis situation.

Cost/benefit ratio. The *cost/benefit ratio* of a research study is determined by calculating the costs and benefits and then deciding whether the costs outweigh the benefits or vice versa. Costs can be of many kinds—the researcher's energy, time consumed, money spent, frustration, ill health, damaged social relations, and neglect of other responsibilities. Benefits can also be diverse, such as the research problem satisfactorily solved, personal satisfaction for a job well done, reduced frustration and worry, other people's admiration and gratitude, and enhanced social relations. Because costs and benefits are so variegated, there is no common coin—no common denominator—to apply in calculating a cost/benefit ratio. Hence, the computation requires an imprecise sort of mental algebra by which the researcher decides whether pursuing the proposed topic will be worth the trouble.

- A nursery school teacher read a series of research studies about the long-term effect of Head Start programs on preschool children's subsequent academic progress. The purpose of such programs was to offer educational enrichment activities to three- and four-year-olds who were from economically or socially disadvantaged homes. The programs were designed to give such children experiences similar to those that prepared children from more affluent families to succeed well in school. According to several of the studies, the children from Head Start programs, when they entered kindergarten and first grade, initially performed better than did children from similar home backgrounds who had not participated in Head Start. However, by the time the Head Start pupils reached fourth or fifth grade, their initial advantage seemed to disappear, resulting in their succeeding no better than their non-Head-Start agemates. Thus, Head Start graduates increasingly lagged behind classmates from more advantaged homes.

The teacher surmised that the apparent deterioration of Head Start's influence was the result of insufficient home support for children's academic progress throughout the elementary-school years. She noted that children whose parents were more affluent and had more advanced education routinely received more experiences that fostered school success than did children from less favored families. She believed the Head Start graduates could progress well if they could also be given similar experiences throughout their elementary school years. As a way to test this hypothesis, she outlined the main features of a *cooperative home-school support program* that might help children maintain the advantage they had initially received from their Head Start preparation. Her plan would require that she follow the children from first grade to fifth grade in order to monitor the home-school-cooperation portion of the plan and to assess the children's academic progress. However, upon considering the advantages and disadvantages of the proposal, she finally abandoned it. She decided that the costs outweighed the benefits. If her program did succeed as she had hoped, her status in the field of early childhood education would be much enhanced when she published her results. But she felt that she could not afford to dedicate five years to the project. Although she considered her plan both important and feasible, the personal sacrifice—in terms of time, money, and energy—was not worth the expense.

Feasibility. The feasibility of a contemplated research topic is judged by answering the question: Is it reasonable to assume that all of the activities that the research plan requires can be performed satisfactorily? Or, stated differently, to what extent are the intended information-gathering and interpretation procedures practicable?

- A state legislature passed a law requiring that public schools include the majority of the state's students with disabilities in regular classrooms. To meet the standards of this legislation, children and youths who formerly had been educated in segregated classrooms or schools designed to serve only students with disabilities would now spend all or most of their time in regular classes, along with their peers who did not have visual, auditory, mobility, behavioral, or cognitive impairments. As the program was implemented, many teachers of regular classes complained about the problems they experienced trying to meet the requirements of the legislation to accommodate the needs of students with significant disabilities, and, at the same time, give proper attention to the needs of their non-disabled classmates.

  A special-education teacher was curious about (a) the type of evidence on which the state legislators had based their voting for the mainstreaming law, (b) where the legislators had obtained such evidence, and (c) the legislators' motives in passing the law. Therefore, he proposed to apply for a sabbatical leave from his school in order to carry out an interview survey of state legislators to find answers to his concerns. However, when he discussed the proposal with the principal of his school, the principal asked him, "From the perspective of a state senator, what would be the advantage of spending time defending one's voting record to a teacher who would then probably report that information in a professional journal or as a newspaper article?

"And assuming that the senator would want to know ahead of time the questions the teacher would present in the interview, what political risks might the senator see in being asked for the evidence—pro and con—about the desirability of the kind of mainstreaming that the law required? How willing might the senator be to answer questions about the reliability of the sources of his evidence? In short, I doubt that you could get the cooperation needed for carrying out such a project."

When the teacher pondered these questions, he decided that the task he had set for himself was not feasible. Even though it seemed like a good idea, he concluded that he could not successfully "pull it off."

Phrasing Topics Precisely

Once a teacher has chosen a research topic, a useful next step is to decide on an appropriate way to the phrase the topic. As illustrated in Chapter 1, the simplest, most direct way to express the purpose of a research project is to state the questions that the project is supposed to answer. Usually it is helpful to organize the questions in the form of an outline, with minor questions subsumed under major ones. Here are two examples in which an overarching major question that identifies the general purpose of a study is followed by minor questions that specify constituent details of the plan. The teacher's research task, then, is that of discovering convincing answers to the questions.

1. In what ways do members of the community's religious organizations influence the teaching methods and subject-matter content of the public high schools' sex-education programs?
   1.1 Which community groups qualify as religious organizations?
   1.2 Which members of religious organizations influence high schools' sex-education programs?
   1.3 What methods do such members use to affect sex-education programs?
   1.4 How successfully have different groups and their methods influenced sex-education programs?
   1.5 What conditions determine the degree of influence that religious organizations exert? That is, under what circumstances do organizations exert much influence, and under what circumstances do they exert little or no influence?

2. In Foothill County schools over the past century, what significant changes have occurred in the development of home-economics education?
   2.1 What is meant by home-economics education, and how has the meaning changed over the years?
   2.2 How has the school system changed over the past century?

2.3 What significant events have accounted for developmei economics curricula?

2.4 Who have been key individuals in the developmen economics programs during different eras?

2.5 What problems have occurred in the development of the programs, and how have those problems been dealt with?

2.6 How has the enrollment in home economics changed over the years?

2.7 What are likely future trends in the development of the home economics programs, and what are the forces behind such trends?

Creating Definitions

A further step toward stating the research topic precisely (and this step is often neglected) is that of creating clear definitions of key words and phrases which refer to concepts at the core of the research project. Those concepts must be clearly understood by both the researcher and recipients of the final research report if the investigation is to be conducted with proper care and if the methods and outcomes are to be unmistakably grasped by readers. Some of the most basic terms that call for definitions are found in the research study's title or in its topic question. In the following examples, each key expression that needs to be defined is underlined. The reason the expressions require clear definitions is that, if the expressions are vague, different readers may bring incorrect meanings to the terms. Therefore, unless the researcher specifies which meanings are intended in the reported study, readers may misunderstand important aspects of the research.

How well do students at different age levels understand historical time?

How reliable and valid is the Kaermer Science Test Series for evaluating pupils' science achievement?

What federal grants are available for developing novel classroom-instruction projects?

The task of providing precise definitions can be illustrated with four popular ways to explain terms: (a) offering a synonym, (b) providing a concise, abstract, dictionary-type description of the researcher's intended meaning, (c) citing a life-like example that enables the author and readers to share a clarifying experience, and (d) defining a term by describing the operations performed in evaluating the concept's presence.

Synonyms. Merely offering a synonym is rarely sufficient for clarifying an ambiguous term. A reader is not helped much if the author explains that *understand* means *comprehend*, that *evaluating* means *assessing*, or that *achievement* means *attainment*. However, synonyms are occasionally useful when they offer a specific term for a more general one that ome readers may not be able to interpret accurately. For instance, *federal* can be recast as "United States government" and *classroom projects* can be equated with "classroom teaching procedures." Synonyms are also appropriate for explaining the meaning of foreign-language expressions, such as *précis* means a "a concise summary" and *quid pro quo* means "the exchange of one thing in return for another."

Brief, abstract definitions. A sentence or two is often sufficient to clarify the intent of a term.

The expression *students at different age levels* refers to "the individuals enrolled in social-studies classes in grades 4, 8, and 12 of Capital City public schools."

Historical time, as intended in this study, refers to (a) the sequence in which events have occurred in the past, (b) the amount of time between events, and (c) the labels applied to different time segments (day, week, month, year, decade, century, millennium).

The term *test reliability* refers to (a) how similar the scores students earn on a test one day will be to the scores they earn if they take that test again a day or so later (test-retest reliability) or (b) the extent to which the items on a test all measure for the same type of skill or knowledge (internal consistency, often called split-half reliability or alternate-form reliability).

Test validity means that a test accurately measures the traits, skills, or knowledge that it is supposed to measure.

The *Kaermer Science Test Series* is a set of four multiple-choice achievement tests designed to assess pupils' (grades 3 through 6) understanding of science facts and concepts relating to physics, botany, zoology, astronomy, and geology.

The expression *pupils' science achievement* refers to how well children in grades 3 through 6 at Hilton Elementary School have mastered the skills and concepts of the science curriculum for those grade levels.

Novel classroom instruction projects are "unusual teaching procedures for use in elementary and secondary school classes."

Grants are funds given to school systems or to individual schools that submit applications that fulfill the conditions described in particular educational-aid legislation.

The word *available* in the phrase "federal grants are available" means that (a) the way of applying for funds to develop novel classroom-instruction projects is advertised in government publications, in education magazines and journals, and on the U. S. Department of Education's Internet website and (b) there are sufficient funds to accommodate all projects that fulfill the application requirements.

Life-like examples. The purpose of life-like examples is to explain the meaning of an expression by describing a daily-life event that readers can recognize.

nals, curriculum guidebooks) and thus have not been generally available to teachers.

Where to Locate Definitions

From the viewpoint of the people who read a research report, definitions of key terms should appear at the place in the report that the definitions are needed for accurately understanding the meanings the researcher intends.   Therefore, it will be desirable to place some definitions very early in the report but to locate others at later junctures.

For instance, imagine that we have conducted a study to answer the question "What are the characteristics of religious education in Lincoln City's public and private elementary-school classrooms?"   It is important at the outset of the research report for readers to understand the meanings the author assigns to the words *religious* and *education*, so the report might begin this way:

> The purpose of this investigation has been to identify the nature of religious education in Lincoln City's public and private elementary-school classrooms.   And because there is no universal agreement about the meaning of either *religion* or *education*, it is useful at the outset for readers to recognize how those words are intended throughout this report.
>
> First, writers who think of *religion* as broadly inclusive often define the word as "the collective expression of human values" or "a system of values or preferences—an inferential values system."   Such definitions are so broad that they encompass not only the belief systems of Christianity, Islam, and Judaism but also those of democracy, communism, and even anarchism.
>
> Second, other writers place far greater limitations on *religion*, proposing that the word should be restricted to identifying a conceptual scheme that is an integrated system of specified components, including the nature of a supreme being or of gods (theology), the origin and condition of the universe (cosmology), rules governing human relations (ethics, morals), the proper behavior of people toward superhuman powers (rites, rituals, worship), the nature of knowledge and its proper sources (epistemology), and the goal of life (teleology).   Under this second sort of definition, Christianity, Islam, and Judaism are religions but democracy, communism, and anarchism are not.   The second of these definitions of *religion* is the one intended in this report.
>
> Just as *religion* has been defined in various ways by different writers, so has *education*.   In its broadest sense, *education* can be equated with *learning*.   And *learning* can be defined as "changes in mental processes and overt behavior as a result of experience."   However, for the purposes of this study of religious education in elementary-school classrooms, *education* is defined in a narrower sense to mean "the activity carried on by a society's institutions of systematic, planned instruction."   Such a definition eliminates from consideration kinds of learning informally acquired during people's daily social interaction, as through their conversations in the family or through models of behavior displayed by their companions.   It also eliminates learning via

the incidental use of libraries, bookshops, newspapers, and recreational radio and television.

When the above preferred definitions are combined, they identify the realm of *religious education* as that of "systematic, planned instruction in beliefs about the nature of the cosmos and supreme powers, about rites and worship, about personal moral values and the ethics of human relations, and about the meaning and goal of life."

Two features of this introduction are particularly worth noting. First, the definitions draw on more than one way to explain the author's meanings, including (a) brief, abstract, dictionary-like statements (*rules governing human relations*), (b) synonyms (*ethics, morals*), and (c) life-like examples (*recreational radio and television*). Second, the definitions not only tell what a term *does mean* but also what it *does not mean* that readers might mistakenly believe are within the term's domain (*democracy, communism, anarchism*).

Whereas definitions crucial for introducing readers to what a research project is all about can properly appear quite early in the research report, other definitions will not be needed until a later point in the document. Let's assume that in this study of religion in the classroom the researcher intends to collect information through interviews with teachers and through content analyses of textbooks that classes use. Both of these methods call for operational definitions—descriptions of exactly how the interviews will be conducted (with whom, where, when, the questions posed, the method of recording responses) and how the textbooks' content will be analyzed and the recorded. For readers, those definitions are most convenient if they appear at the places in the report that the methods of data-collection are introduced.

Starting to Write

I imagine that most people who are new to the business of doing research expect that the task of writing the report is best left till the end of the entire research process. That is, they expect that writing should start only after all of the data have been collected, classified, and interpreted. However, in my experience, writing a draft of the first section of the report very early in the game can yield valuable dividends.

Typically, the role assigned to the opening portion of a research report (the first section of an article or the first chapter of a book) is that of explaining to readers the aim of the research, the general way the research was conducted, and how the report is organized. Therefore, it is useful for the author to adopt a reader's perspective and to ask "In the report's early pages, by what phrasing and in what sequence, would I—if I were a reader—most easily grasp the purpose of the research and understand, in general, how the project was carried out?"

By way of illustration, here is one way we might start the opening paragraphs of our hypothetical study of how well students understand historical time. Such a beginning can be written as soon as we have decided on our research questions and our method of gathering data—and before we have actually started to collect information and interpret it. Although this trial draft is written at the outset of the project, prior to our collecting any data, it is written in past tense, the way it would be when the project had been completed.

Students' Conceptions of Historical Times

As infants develop through childhood and adolescence into adulthood, they encounter a growing variety of meanings for the word *time*. This diversity of meanings is reflected in such expressions as *being on time, spending time, wasting time, investing time, lost time, time out, overtime, time payments, timeless*, and *time of your life*. The growing child also learns about *past times, good times, bad times, memorable times, old times, future times*, and more. One sort of time that increasingly demands students' attention as their school years advance is *historical time*.

Past research on people's conceptions of historical time has supported the common-sense observation that children's grasp of historical time improves with the passing years. The fourth-grade child's notion of historical time is expected to be more accurate than the kindergarten child's, and a tenth-grader's understanding is expected to be better than a fourth-grader's.

The research described in this article is intended to be a contribution to the body of knowledge about children's and youths' understanding of historical time by answering two questions:

(1) How accurate, on the average, are the conceptions of historical time of fourth-graders, eighth-graders, and twelfth-graders in the public schools of a medium-sized U.S. American city?

(2) Within each grade level (4, 8, 12), what is the range of differences among students in their understanding of historical time?

Answers to the questions were derived by means of the researcher (a) assigning students in the three grades to locate on a time line a series of specified events they had studied in their social-studies or history class and (b) analyzing the results of the students' work in order to determine the average accuracy of understanding at each grade level as well as the range between the most accurate and least accurate students' conceptions within each grade.

The following account of the research is presented in six sections: (a) past studies of historical time, (b) the time-line test, (c) the sample of students, (d) administering the test, (e) the compiled results, and (f) implications for teaching about historical time.

Writing such a draft early in the research process forces the author to foresee the components of the project before the data are collected and analyzed. Such a preview can thus alert the teacher/researcher to important aspects of the study that otherwise might have been overlooked if left until late in the research process. For example, some people hasten to collect data before they consider how the data are to be classified and analyzed, with the result that they can arrive at the interpretation stage of the study lacking some of the information they need for answering the research questions.

Planning Guide

To furnish readers an opportunity to make immediate use of the contents of Chapters 2 through 9, a planning guide is placed at the end of each chapter. By carrying out the activities suggested in the guides, readers are able to prepare a detailed plan for a research project that they might sometime wish to conduct.

Here is a sequence of tasks that provide readers practice in applying the concepts and procedures described in the present chapter.

1. Write three questions you might like to answer by doing research. In each question, underline every word or phrase that you believe needs to be defined if readers are to understand the meanings you intend for those expressions.
2. For each underlined expression in the three questions, offer a definition in the form that you believe makes your intended meanings clear.
3. Arrange your three questions in the order of their desirability by applying to them such appraisal criteria as (a) persuasive outcome, (b) cost-benefit, (c) feasibility, or (d) other standards that you consider important, such as the contribution the research results can make to improving classroom teaching or the likelihood that readers would find the project interesting.
4. For the research question that you have judged to be the most desirable, write a hypothetical beginning of an envisioned article or book chapter—a beginning that you consider appropriate for the kind of audience for which your report would be intended.

3

Consulting the Literature

The term *the literature*, as intended throughout this book, refers to sources of published material that can be useful in the conduct of research. The most familiar, time-honored components of *the literature* have been books, encyclopedias, academic journals, magazines, newspapers, almanacs, atlases, brochures, and newsletters. But of particular note, over the past two decades the ways of finding information have been dramatically increased by the advent of the computer-based Internet and its World Wide Web.

The dual purpose of this chapter is (a) to identify how the literature can contribute to the success of research projects and (b) to suggest efficient ways of locating information, extracting it, and organizing the results. The chapter is divided into four sections that explain what to hunt for in the literature, ways to survey the print literature, how to search the World Wide Web, and useful databases.

What to Hunt for in the Literature

Exploring the literature can be a useful activity at any stage of the research process. At the beginning, when a person is first trying to settle on a topic to investigate, the literature can help by revealing potential topics and showing what kinds of studies have been conducted on those topics in the past. Next, at the stage of defining key terms, the literature can provide examples of other researchers' definitions. The literature can also suggest methods for collecting data and can identify the advantages and disadvantages of those methods. Furthermore, at the stage of organizing data, descriptions of past studies can provide useful information about data-classification systems and statistical analysis. The literature can also suggest ways to interpret research results, ways to apply the results in solving classroom problems, and how to disseminate the research report.

Consequently, the task of hunting in the literature is most efficiently pursued when researchers have clearly in mind the stage of the research process that is the focus of the hunt and have decided what questions they are trying to answer at that juncture. Reading an entire book or article completely, in the hope of finding something worthwhile, is usually a waste of time. The hunt is typically most economical when it focuses on selected parts of a book or article or the World Wide Web, as illustrated below.

Ways to Survey Print Literature

The term *print literature* refers to such traditional sources of information as books, encyclopedias, journals, magazines, and newspapers. Print literature can also take the form of microfilm or microfiche reproductions. Three approaches to surveying print literature are illustrated in the following cases that involve the stages of (a) delineating the domain of the research project, (b) designing a method of gathering data, and (c) locating a publishing outlet. (Readers already skilled in surveying print literature may wish to skip this section and jump ahead to the sections on helpful data bases when searching the World Wide Web.)

Case 1: Delineating the Research Project's Domain

In a county whose principal industry was that of growing and exporting fruit, the superintendent of schools offered a high school social-studies teacher a one-semester sabbatical leave to conduct a study that might help the school district cope with the problem of many pupils entering and leaving school at various times during the school year because their parents were itinerant fruit-crop workers. Such families came to the county during the season of heavy demand for fruit pickers and cannery workers, then left when the season was over. Their children were thus shuttled into and out of school at times determined by the fruit industry's demands.

The two-part question that guided the teacher's research was: "In an agricultural region, what classroom-management and instruction problems are caused by pupils from seasonal-labor families entering and leaving school at various times during the school year? What are the apparent consequences of those problems, and what methods can be used to cope with them?"

The teacher decided that the data-collection stage of the project would involve two sorts of activity—a literature search and a survey of the types and frequency of problems in the county's schools.

Establishing a code system. To prepare for the literature search, the teacher identified four of the project's phases that she would write about in her final report. The phases were those of:

- Defining the domain of the study by first identifying *various causes* of irregular school attendance, then centering attention on the *specific cause* that particularly interested her—seasonal-work families entering and leaving the community during the school year.
- Identifying *types* of classroom problems associated with the irregular school attendance of pupils from seasonal-work families.
- Identifying *effects* or *consequences* that the classroom-management and instruction problems produce for pupils, teachers, administrators, and educational-support personnel (bus drivers, counselors, cafeteria workers, attendance officers).
- Identifying *solutions* for the problems, including the success rate of each solution and the conditions that apparently influenced how well a solution succeeded.

These four phases would then serve as categories for coding material collected during the literature search. That is, to facilitate her later task of composing the research report, the teacher intended to use code words for indicating in which section of her final report the notes or quotations from the literature would be used. The five code words were GEN-CAUSE, SPECIF-CAUSE, TYPE, EFFECT, SOLUTION. Therefore, whenever she examined a book chapter, journal article, or newspaper report, she could jot notes on a 3-by-5-inch card, then write at the top of the card the code word indicating the category of her later research report to which the notes applied. In addition to the code word, she would write the name of the author of the chapter or article, the publication year, and the page numbers of the material she summarized. Here is an example:

GEN-CAUSE   *Lenton, 2001, pp. 121-124*

In a New Mexico rural school district, irregular pupil attendance resulted primarily from pupils' illness, from delinquency (cutting classes), and from families traveling because of seasonal-labor demands or to attend family gatherings in Mexico or other parts of the Southwestern U.S.

Then, on a separate 3-by-5-inch card, she would write the complete identification of the journal article by Jason Lenton that was the source of her notes.   That bibliography card—together with similar cards specifying the other references she consulted—would be used in building the list of references that would appear at the end of her final report.

Bibliog

Lenton, J. T. (2001). Attendance and drop-out problems in a rural school district. School Counseling Review, 27 (4), 120-127.

By coding her note cards, the researcher simplified her ultimate task of writing the research report.   At the final writing stage, as she prepared each new section of the report, she merely had to collect all of the cards that bore the same code word and arrange them in a sequence that enabled her to compose a narrative that made sense to readers.

Using the library. The literature search would be conducted in the library of the nearby state university. To prepare for her library visit, the researcher made a list of key terms that would guide her hunt. Among the most obvious terms were ones from her original research question—*agricultural region, seasonal labor, classroom-management, instruction problems.* She added to this list other terms associated with concepts in the research question—*itinerant labor, rural schools, school attendance, dropouts, absence, discipline, classroom control, teaching methods,* and *remedial teaching.*

At the library, her first stop was at a computer terminal that was used to display the library's entire list of books and periodicals. Traditionally this station was known as the *card catalog,* consisting of sets of drawers holding 3-by-5-inch cards. Each card described the author, title, publisher, publishing date, and library-call-number of a book. But in recent years, a computer terminal rather than a set of drawers furnishes access to information about the library's holdings. Therefore, the teacher's task of identifying books relevant to her project consisted of entering a key word or phrase into the computer, which then displayed a list of all books related to that word or phrase. For example, entering the term *school attendance* produced a list of 493 publications that bore such titles as *Student and Teacher Absenteeism, Disruptive Events During the High School Years and Educational Attainment,* and *Factors Influencing the Attendance of Spanish-Culture Children in Ramondville Elementary Schools.* The teacher then wrote the titles and call numbers for ten of the most promising titles so she could subsequently find the books in the library stacks and inspect the books' contents. She noted that the call numbers for several of the books were in the LC143 to LC145 range, so she first hunted in that section of the stacks, because she would likely find numerous additional useful volumes there. In effect, identifying several books with similar call numbers suggested that more volumes bearing on school attendance would also be in that same place. Therefore, not only would she find the books whose call numbers she had copied, but she would be able to inspect other books shelved nearby that served her purpose.

In the LC143—LC145 section of the stacks, she began taking each potentially useful book from the shelf and skimming its table of contents and index, hunting for any of her key terms. When, in the table of contents or index, she found one of the terms, she turned to the appropriate pages and skimmed the paragraphs to discover if any of the material was relevant to any of her code words—GEN-CAUSE, SPECIF-CAUSE, TYPE, EFFECT, SOLUTION. Whenever she found a passage that was indeed relevant, she either summarized the passage on a 3-by-5 note card or, if the passage was lengthy (a full page or more), she would photocopy it on one of the library's photocopy machines. Each time she photocopied a passage, she would write on the back of the sheet the information she would need for the bibliography in her final report. When she returned home, she moved the information to a bibliography card.

A few of the books the teacher found contained more useful material than she could conveniently summarize as handwritten notes or as photocopied passages. In these cases, she borrowed the books, taking them home to extract the useful parts at her leisure, either by photocopying portions or summarizing the information on her computer. On each summarized segment, she wrote the code word that indicated where in her final report that segment should prove useful.

In addition to inspecting books, the teacher sought journal and magazine articles relating to her project. Here she used two approaches. First, she searched through two sets of volumes that listed journal articles on education topics—*Education Index* and *Current Index to Journals in Education* (CIJE). Her hunt was again directed by her key terms. Looking under a key term in one of the indexes enabled her to locate the titles of journal articles related to her interest and the names and dates of those periodicals. With this information in hand, she could use the computerized catalog to discover the call numbers of the journals and thereby find the journals in the library stacks. In the same way that she had skimmed the contents of books, she scanned the contents of the journal articles to locate and record information pertinent to her code words.

In summary, the foregoing example illustrates one way of searching the print literature to identify components of the general domain (irregular school attendance) and specific domain (irregular attendance of children from seasonal-labor families) of a research project.

Case 2: Designing a Data-Collecting Process

Two national news reports of students being shot in schools by enraged classmates alerted administrators in a small city school system to question how well local teachers and students were prepared to cope with emergencies. A high-school principal discussed the problem with one of the school's social-studies teachers who was currently pursuing a master's degree in a nearby university. The principal wondered if the school-violence issue might be a suitable topic for the teacher's graduate-degree thesis. The teacher agreed that it would be a suitable topic, and he identified three questions that the research would be expected to answer.

- What regulations or guidelines for dealing with emergencies are furnished to classroom teachers in the city's public schools?
- How do those regulations and guidelines compare with ones in other school districts?
- What opinions about the adequacy of the guidelines are expressed by teachers, students, and parents?

The plan the teacher submitted envisioned a final thesis consisting of six chapters and of subsections within chapters.

Chapter 1: Introduction
    1.1 Types of school emergencies
    1.2 Aims of this research project
    1.3 The research design

Chapter 2: Methods of Data Collection and Analysis
    2.1 Mailed or phoned requests for information
    2.2 Questionnaires
        2.2.1 Types
        2.2.2 Advantages, disadvantages
        2.2.3 Constructing
        2.2.4 Administering
    2.3 Interviews
        2.3.1 Types
        2.3.2 Advantages, disadvantages

This outline served as the teacher's guide to what he should hunt for at the library. How he would proceed can be illustrated with tasks 2.2 and 2.3 in his Chapter 2. At that point in the thesis, he intended to describe the advantages and disadvantages of various types of questionnaires and interviews, then select the types that seemed most suitable for collecting the information he needed in Chapters 3, 4, and 5.

His method of searching the literature involved four steps. First, he pasted a copy of his thesis outline on the inside front cover of a loose-leaf notebook, since he planned to use the numbers in the outline for coding notes that he took during his literature search and he wanted the numbers to be readily available. He intended to take notes on notebook paper rather than on cards, since pages in a notebook seemed easier to handle than loose cards.

Second, he listed key terms that he would use to guide his hunt for relevant publications. The terms included *questionnaires, opinionnaires, interviews, attitude surveys, polling,* and *data collection.*

Third, he consulted the library catalog at the college he attended. But rather than going directly to the library and using a computer terminal to find book titles, he stayed at home and employed his personal computer to reach the library catalog. To accomplish this, he used his computer to contact the college library via the telephone line (by means of a *modem*) and thereby was able to see all of the same information that a computer terminal in the library would provide.

Fourth, with the library's catalog displayed on his home computer screen, he began entering key words. For example, when he typed the word *questionnaires,* he was informed that there were 331 books in the library associated with that word. He could then display the list of books, ten at a time, on his computer screen, select from the list those titles that seemed most promising, and write the titles and their library call numbers in his notebook. Those were the volumes he would later inspect when he visited the library.

Here are four of the ten he choose:

Attitude and Opinion Research: Why You Need It, How to Do It —HN261.A83
The Design and Understanding of Survey Questions — HN29.B45
Questionnaires: Design and Use —BF39 B445
Survey Questions: Handcrafting the Standardized Questionnaire —HN29.C661

When he entered the keyword *interviewing* into the catalog, he found 1,184 book titles. Here are four of the eight he selected from that list:

Interviewing Procedures: A Manual for Survey Interviewers —BF637.I5 A1
Interviewing for Social Scientists: An Introductory Resource —HM526.A75
A Summary of Research Studies of Interviewing Methodology —W2 AN148
Using Structured Interview Techniques —GA 1.2 (Gov Info Microfilm)

Fifth, by scanning the catalog lists at home rather than waiting until he went to the library, the teacher was able to survey the book titles at his convenience, thereby saving time when he visited the library, because upon entering the library he was able to go directly to the proper shelves to inspect the contents of the selected volumes. When he took a book from the shelf, he hunted for his key words in the book's index, then turned to the listed pages to find potentially useful material.

Sixth, when he found passages of value, he wrote a summary of the material in his notebook, placed a code number from his thesis outline in the left margin to indicate the part of his thesis for which the passage was pertinent, and wrote the bibliographic source at the end of the summary.

If a needed passage in a book was long or the teacher wished to quote it exactly, he photocopied the relevant pages, then wrote the thesis code number and the bibliographic source in the top margin of the photocopy.

Here is a typical page in his notebook.

2.2.1 *Questionnaires can have (1) open-ended questions where the respondent must write out an answer or (2) multiple-choice questions where the respondent selects the best answer from several choices or (3) a combination of open-ended and multiple-choice items. (Harris & Harris, 2000, p. 16)*

2.3.1 *Interviews can vary in the degree to which they are structured. Highly structured interviews consist of very specific, focused questions that usually require a rather short, precise answer. Lowly structured (unstructured) interviews involve asking only very general and perhaps vague questions that encourage interviewees to pretty much define for themselves what they are going to talk about. (Blane, 1985, p.47)*

2.2.4 *A problem with mailing questionnaires to respondents is that there is no guarantee that all of the people will fill out the questionnaires and send them back. Therefore, it's best to have the respondents in one place—such as having students in a class—so they feel obligated to complete the questionnaire before leaving the classroom. With mailed questionnaires, always include a stamped, self-addressed envelope in which people can return the completed questionnaire to you. Send a reminder to those who haven't returned their questionnaire. (Garcia, 1992, p. 127)*

2.2.4 *If respondents can read a questionnaire adequately, then let them fill it out themselves. Otherwise, handle it like an interview by reading each question aloud and recording respondents' answers by marking the appropriate items on the questionnaire. (Garcia, 1992, p. 130)*

2.3.2 *Interviewing by phone enables you to cover a lot of respondents in various locations within a short time period. However, if you phone them when they are busy with important activities, you may just antagonize them so they hang up, and you lose them from your sample. (Lamon, 1979, p. 13)*

By following this procedure, the teacher accumulated information for sections 2.2 (Questionnaires) and 2.3 (Interviews) of his thesis outline. That information was in the form (a) of handwritten paragraphs of material in no particular order on page after page of notebook paper and (b) photocopied sheets.

Seventh, upon returning home, he used scissors to cut out each coded summary from his notebook, and he placed each clipping in a manila folder which contained all clippings that bore the same code number. Thus, he had one folder for notes coded 2.2.1, another for notes pertinent to 2.2.2, and so on. By means of such a system, he accumulated in each folder all of the information needed to write about the topic that the code represented.

While scanning the contents of library books, he might have encountered material useful in parts of his thesis other than sections 2.2 and 2.3. So it would be to his advantage—in terms of saving time and bother—to take notes immediately about those matters rather than waiting to record that information later when he would be working specifically on that section of his thesis. For example, while focusing on questionnaires (2.2) and interviews (2.3), he might incidentally come across information about types of emergencies in schools (1.1). Therefore, he would be wise to summarize that passage immediately as an entry among his notes bearing on questionnaires and interviews and to code the passage as 1.1. Therefore, when he returned home, he obviously would know to put that clipping in the folder labeled 1.1.

In conclusion, the researcher in Case 2 made greater use of a computer than did the researcher in Case 1. At the beginning of his hunt, he prepared a tentative outline of his envisioned final report, then used the numbers in the outline as codes identifying where he would locate material he found in his library search. In addition, he accessed the college library's catalog from his personal computer at home, thereby reducing the amount of time he would need to spend in the library.

Case 3: Locating a Publishing Outlet

A junior-high physical-education instructor completed a research project titled *A Comparison of Three Early-Adolescence Physical Fitness Programs* and wanted to find a journal or magazine in which to publish the results. One way to approach this task would be to visit a library in order to inspect academic journals and popular magazines that included articles about the subject of his study. Key terms that would aid him in finding such publications through the library's catalog of periodicals included *physical fitness, physical education, sports, athletics, good health, body building, aerobics, strength,* and *physical endurance.*

When he identified an apparently suitable periodical and found copies of the periodical in the library stacks, he could browse through the articles in order to find ones that addressed physical-fitness programs. He also would be able to discover the style in which each periodical's articles were written and the typical length of articles. If the publication was an academic journal, then on the inside of the front or back cover he might find guidelines describing the desired form of articles submitted for publication and the address to which authors should send their manuscripts. He might also find it useful to inspect the bibliographies or listed references at the end of articles about fitness in order to identify the names of additional publications in the field beyond those that he had already found among this library's holdings.

By such a procedure, the teacher could compile a list of potential outlets for his research report and could send his manuscript to the periodical that appeared to be the most suitable. If the first publisher turned down his manuscript, he would be ready with the addresses of other periodicals to which he could submit the study.

How to Search the World Wide Web

The computer Internet is composed of a great number of large capacity computers around the world that are linked together to furnish a communication system serving many millions of individuals and organizations. The Internet enables people—while at home, in school, in the office, or on a trip—to exchange messages (e-mail), engage in group conversations (chat groups), purchase products, and find information about nearly any topic that one could imagine. The largest portion of the Internet is the World Wide Web, a domain containing millions of *websites*, that is, millions of Internet locations containing information of all kinds. Websites are created by organizations or individuals to give Internet users access to the sort of information that an organization or individual wishes to disseminate. For researchers, the World Wide Web has become an extremely valuable resource. Sitting at home before their computers, teachers can find and copy information from all parts of the world.

The following example demonstrates one way the World Wide Web can be exploited by a person doing research on classroom topics. Our illustrative case is that of an elementary school teacher, who is a member of the school district's curriculum advisory committee, planning a study entitled *Primary-Grade Pupils' Computer Skills* for the committee's use. The questions the project is designed to answer are:

At each primary-grade level (kindergarten through grade three):

1. What computer skills do pupils command at the beginning of the school year and what skills do they command at the end of the school year?
2. What formal instruction in computer skills do pupils receive in class during the school year?
3. What informal opportunities to learn computer skills do pupils receive (a) in class and (b) outside of class?

The teacher intends to answer those questions by gathering information from the primary-grade classes of four elementary schools in the school district. However, at the outset of her project, in order to profit from similar studies conducted elsewhere, she conducts a review of the professional literature. An important part of her review is a search of the World Wide Web. The following paragraphs describe the equipment she uses to access the Web and the steps she adopts for locating and recording information she considers potentially helpful for her project.

Needed Equipment

To carry out her search, the teacher requires:

- A personal computer equipped with a *modem* (a device for connecting the computer to a telephone line). In computers of recent vintage, modems are already installed by the computer manufacturer. In older computers, a modem must be purchased and attached by the computer owner.
- An Internet service provider (ISP), which is a commercial company (such as *America Online, AT&T Worldnet,* or *Earthlink*) or a nonprofit organization (university, school system, or government agency) that provides access to the Internet. In our example, the teacher uses a nearby university's ISP.
- A *browser,* which is a software program in the computer that equips the user to navigate around the Internet to find things of interest. Among the more popular browsers are Netscape and Explorer. In recent models of computers, a browser is installed at the factory so it is already available when the computer is purchased.
- Because there are so many millions of *websites* or *web pages* to visit on the World Wide Web, it is useful as well to employ one or more *search engines.* A search engine is a computer program that uses keywords for exploring millions of sites on the Web. Popular search engines bear such names as *Google, AltaVista, Teoma,* and *Yahoo.*

With such equipment available, the teacher is ready to begin her search for past studies of children's computer skills.

The Search Procedure

She starts with key terms related to her research plan, including *computer skills, computers in school,* and *computers in primary grades.* When she turns on her computer, among the dozen icons she sees on the screen is the one representing the university's ISP.

To open the ISP, she moves the mouse to touch the floating arrow onto the icon. When the server opens, she taps the arrow on the Explorer browser icon. After the browser opens, she is ready to enter either the name or the web address of the search engine she wishes to use.

Here are some search-engine web addresses she has available.

Google	http://www.google.com/
Lycos	http://lycos.cs.cmu.edu/
HotBot	http: //hotbot.lycos.com/
Excite	http://www.excite.com/
Ask Jeeves	http://www.ask.com/
Teoma	http: //www.teoma.com/
AltaVista	http://www.altavista.com/

Two engines designed particularly for children to use are:

Yahooligans	http://www.yahooligans.com/
Ask Jeeves Kids	http://www.ajkids.com/

The address that she types into the blank space is Google's. She then taps the **Go** rectangle with the mouse's arrow.

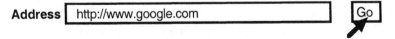

As she inspects the list of websites that now appear on the screen, she moves the arrow to the first in the list, which brings up the Google home page, with a blank space into which a key word or phrase can be entered. The first key term that she types in that space is *computers in schools,* then taps the *Google Search* ellipse.

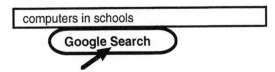

In a few seconds, the page listing *computers-in-schools* websites appears on the screen (10 items per page). A note at the top of the frame informs her that the total number of relevant websites is about 1,200,000. Because the task of completely inspecting such a list would be unduly burdensome, she tries to reduce the total by entering a more restricted key term—*computers, primary schools*—which yields a list of about 395,000 sites. That number is still overwhelming, so she decides to restrict the hunt even more by trying separate grade levels. When she types *computers, kindergarten*, a list of 154,000 options appears at the rate of ten per page.

The teacher now inspects the items on the first page to see if their titles and short descriptions seem useful for her project. She does the same for the next few pages that appear on the screen. Among the items she opens to read is a website prepared by a school principal for a professional conference, showing precisely how computers were being used in the kindergarten of the principal's school. The description includes color photos illustrating each part of the explanation. The teacher now uses the *copy* function on her computer to copy passages from several pages of that website and uses the *paste* function to add them to a file from her own word-processing program. She titles the file *computers, kindergarten*. To accompany that material, she types the address of that website (http://www.siec.k12.in.us/~west/slides/integrate/). The address will be needed later for the bibliography in her dissertation if she refers to that website's material in her research report.

She follows this same procedure in order to record potentially useful passages from additional websites. That is, she (a) opens a web page that looks promising, (b) inspects the contents, (c) uses her word-processing program's *copy* function to lift useful passages from the site, (d) uses the program's *paste* function to insert those passages into the file labeled *computers, kindergarten* and (e) attaches the web address to the pasted passage. By this process, she accumulates a host of information about how computer skills are taught in a variety of kindergartens. But she does not attempt to survey all 154,000 of the *computers, kindergarten* websites. Rather, she finds enough material to suit her needs from among the first 20 pages that appear on the screen (representing 200 sites).

Next, she enters the term *computers, first grade* into the *Google Search* blank, thereby locating a list of 561,000 sites. In an attempt to reduce the number of sites, she changes her key term to *computer skills, first grade*, which produces around 516,000 websites. As an illustration of the sorts of brief descriptions offered for each site, here are two from the *computer-skills, first-grade* list.

First Grade Computer Skills. COMPETENCY GOAL 1. The learner will understand important issues of a technology-based society and will exhibit ethical behavior in ...

THE ABC's of READING SOFTWARE ... songs. This software teaches first-grade reading skills but may ... progression in oral reading skills. 5-year-old Timmy ..."talk" to a computer. What would our ...

Then, following the same procedure that she used for computers in kindergartens, the teacher copies potentially helpful material about computers in Grade 1 and pastes that material in a word-processing file titled *computers, first grade.* Here is a portion of that file.

---

computers, first grade

Source: **SNEISD First Grade Technology Competencies and Performance Descriptions.** Online. Available: http://www.northeast.isd.tenet. edu/oakm/Computers/first.html

The first grader will:
- *create, type from keyboard, save*— (use word processing for word recogni-tion, including using the keyboard for input and saving the file to a disk).
- *identify and use paint tools*—(produce a drawing based upon teacher di-rections or use the drawing tools to illustrate original compositions).
- *begin email communications*—(with teacher guidance, will explore email communications).
- *learn finger positions*—(learn correct finger positions and will begin to use the correct fingers to type).

Source: **Computer/Technology Skills Curriculum.** (North Carolina Public Schools website). Online. Available: http://www.ncpublicschools. org/curriculum/computer.skills/1.html

Competency Goal 1. The learner will understand important issues of a tech-nology-based society and will exhibit ethical behavior in the use of com-puter and other technologies.
    1.1 Identify uses of technology at home and at school. (SI)
    1.2 Discuss ownership of computer-created work. (SI)
    1.3 Identify physical components of a computer system. (SI)
    1.4 Identify the Internet as a source of information. (T)

Competency Goal 2. The learner will demonstrate knowledge and skills in the use of computer and other technologies.
    2.1 Identify and discuss fundamental computer terms. (SI)
    2.2 Locate and use letters, numbers, and special keys on a keyboard. (KU/WP/DTP)

2.3 Identify basic word processing terms. (KU/WP/DTP)

2.4 KU/WP/DTP)

2.5 Participate in the creation of a class multimedia sequential/linear story.

The teacher also searches the World Wide Web for information about *computer skills, second grade* (397,000 sites) and *computer skills, third grade* (303,000 sites). During the process of inspecting the lists generated by each of the key terms, she recognizes that many of the entries offer nothing useful for her study, a fact that she can usually recognize from the brief descriptions on the list of websites. Therefore, she does not bother to open those sites in order to analyze them in detail. For instance, here are three useless items from the *computer-skills, third-grade* list.

Plenty Coups - Student Work... I began as an instructional aide. I have since taught first grade, third grade, fifth grade, computer skills, and art. I graduated from Western Montana College.

Where to find information online about: university cd-roms, ... to Find Software Skills and Basic Videos ... beginning calculus Dealers third grade Links ... Deals first grade math beginning ... Internet Auction Computer Auction Adult ...

List of Faculty and Staff... Parker Montgomery School, Computer Skills/ Chess, Sharon Moore.   French Kate Mortimer, Art.   Kay Morton, Drama. Rose Neily, Physical Education.   Colleen Paquet, Third Grade

After she has collected the material from the World Wide Web and placed it in word-processing files, the teacher can adopt a coding system—like the ones described on pages 27 and 33—that identifies where in her research report each portion of the material might be of use. An appropriate code number can be typed at the top of each set of material or else the files can be printed out and a relevant code written by hand in the left margin beside the paragraph to which that code applies.

In summary, as illustrated throughout the above discussion, the Internet can be a teacher's valuable ally in the conduct of research.

Useful Databases

The task of searching for information in the Internet is greatly facilitated by databases that list sources of information in particular fields of knowledge. The following are five examples of the many databases available to computer users who have access to public libraries, school libraries, or college and university libraries that subscribe to database services.

Academic Search Elite contains full-text versions (not just summaries) of articles from 2,035 journals, including journals in the social sciences, humanities, education, computer sciences, engineering, physics, chemistry, language & linguistics, arts & literature, medical sciences, ethnic studies, and more. Many of the entries are searchable or are scanned-in-color for easy identification of key terms.

ERIC (Educational Resources Information Center) is advertised as the world's largest source of education information. The database contains more than one million abstracts of education-related documents and journal articles, with the collection updated monthly on the Internet and quarterly on CD-ROMs.

MasterFILE Premier, a database designed specifically for public libraries, furnishes access to information on a broad range of topics, including full-text articles from more than 1,840 journals, plus abstracts of over 2,780 journals from over the past two decades. Additional database contents are 5,000 Magill's book reviews and more than 1,000 original American historical documents.

Newspaper Source provides full-text coverage of 212 regional U.S. newspapers, major international newspapers, syndicated columns, and television and radio transcripts. There are also abstracts of articles from such major national newspapers as *The New York Times* and *The Washington Post.*

Primary Search is designed specifically for elementary school libraries. It furnishes full-text articles from more than 50 elementary-school magazines and 100 pamphlets as well as access to the American Heritage Children's Dictionary.

Some search tools compile results from several search engines and thereby include multiple types of databases. One such meta-tool available in thousands of libraries around the globe is EBSCOhost, touted as the world's most prolific aggregator of full-text journals, magazines, and several other sources. Another meta-tool is the ProQuest subscription service, accessible from libraries in more than 100 countries. Users of ProQuest can view the contents of 4,000 newspapers and periodicals, over a million dissertations, and a wide range of other content.

In the realm of Internet searches, the expression *Boolean logic* refers to the logical relationship among the words used in conducting a search. The Boolean system is named after its inventor, the 19th century British mathematician George Boole (1815-1864). Such Internet search engines as Google, Teoma, Alta Vista, HotBot, and WebCrawler provide for Boolean operations. In the Boolean system, the three most basic terms (called *operators*) are the words <u>AND</u>, <u>OR</u>, and <u>NOT</u>.

To illustrate, imagine that we are interested in finding records on the Internet that concern the relationship between poverty and crime. If we entered just the word *poverty* into the Google search engine, we would come up with about 8,740,000 records, and entering just *crime* would produce around 21,400,000. But if we insert the term *poverty AND crime* we reduce the number of sources to 1,230,000—that is, to only those records that are concerned with the connection between poverty and crime. Therefore, using *AND* rather than entering our two key words separately has saved us the bother of generating millions of entries that would be of no use in our research.

Next, consider the operator *OR*. Using *OR* enables us to find information about web sources that could be known by either of two terms, such as *preschool* and *kindergarten*. If we enter just *preschool* into the Teoma search engine, we find about 1,683,00 websites, while using just *kindergarten* produces 2,087,000. But entering the expression *preschool OR kindergarten* expands our potentially useful sources to around 3,770,000.

Now assume that we wish to locate web pages that contain information about *school administrators*, but we don't want to be bothered with pages that include *school principals*. In order to avoid material about *principals*, we employ the operator *NOT*. Using the Teoma search engine, we enter the expression *"school administrators" NOT "school principals"* and thereby find about 9,500 websites rather than the 229,000 that would result from entering only "school administrators."

In addition to the *AND, OR,* and *NOT* operators, the Boolean approach to web searching can involve additional terms (such as *ADJACENT, WITH, NEAR, FOLLOWED BY*), enabling us to focus our hunt more precisely on what we need for our particular research project. Those additional operators, and how to use them, are typically explained in the engine's *advanced-search* option that shows up when the engine is first opened.

A convenient way to learn the Boolean system is to work through one of the tutorials found on the Internet, such as the following:

http://camellia.shc.edu/literacy/tablesversion/lessons/lesson4/bool
    ean.htm
http://florin.syr.edu/webarch/searchpro/boolean_tutorial.html
http://library.albany.edu/internet/boolean.html
http://www.lscc.cc.fl.us/library/guides/bolsea.htm

In addition, a concise guide to the function of each Boolean term is offered on the following website:

http://catalog.loc.gov/help/boolean.htm

Planning Guide

The following activities provide readers an opportunity to apply the contents of this chapter to either an imagined or an actual research project.

1. For a study that you might like to conduct, state the research question (or questions) that the project would be designed to answer. Next, envision the sequence of sections into which your final report could be divided, and cast these sections as an outline, such as the outline on pages 30 and 31 of this chapter. If you intend your report to take the form of an entire book, then each major section can be described as a chapter. But if the report is to be an article or a chapter in a book, the sections can be seen as the successive parts of the article or chapter. Now select one of those sections as the focus of a library search and create key words or phrases that can direct your review of the literature.

   Visit a library and, with your key terms as your guide, hunt in the library's catalog of books for titles that you believe might contain information relevant to your research project.

   Take each selected book from the shelf and look for your key terms in the table of contents and index. In addition, inspect the titles of other volumes on nearby shelves on the chance of finding other books that may contain pertinent material. Scan the indexes of those volumes.

   When you find information useful for your project, either (a) write a summary on a note card or notebook paper or (b) photocopy the passage if you wish to have a lengthy direct quotation from the source. In addition, on the note card write (a) the code number that identifies the part of your report outline to which the selected information applies and (b) the source of the information, including the number of the page on which the information appears. Also, prepare a reference card recording the complete bibliographical information about the book from which you have drawn the material.

   By carrying through this activity, you now should have in hand much of the information needed for writing the section of your report that you chose as the focus of this literature-search exercise.

2. Activity 1 focuses attention on searching books for information. As Activity 2, carry out the same series of steps as the above for locating useful material in periodicals and newspapers.

3. This exercise concerns the use of the World Wide Web. For your envisioned research project, conduct a search of the Web by means of one or more search engines. Use key terms to locate appropriate

websites, and copy potentially helpful passages into a word-processing file. Attach to each passage the title of the material you have copied, along with its web address, which you will need for your report's bibliography, in the event that you use the material in your project.

4

Research Methods—Qualitative

The expression *research methods*, as used throughout this book, refers to general approaches to gathering and presenting information. Research methods are typically identified by such terms as *historical, biographical, experience-narrative, ethnographic, activity-analysis, survey, correlational,* and *experimental*. Within each method, particular devices are used for collecting information, including such devices as *content analyses, observations, questionnaires, interviews,* and *tests*.

People who speak about research methods often distinguish between *qualitative* and *quantitative* approaches. As those terms are generally used, quantitative research involves amounts, which are usually cast in the form of statistics—frequencies, percentages, percentiles, arithmetic means, standard deviations, correlation coefficients, and the like. In contrast, qualitative research typically involves descriptions of people, places, and events without much concern for amounts, so that statistical comparisons are not involved. Here are titles of studies that might be classsified under each type.

Qualitative:
> *A History of Ability Grouping in Elementary Schools*
> *Lettie Mortensen, School Mistress*
> *An Approach to Teaching Acrylic Portraiture*
> *Life in a Teen Cheerleaders Team*

Quantitative:
> *Teachers' Opinions of Statewide Achievement Tests*
> *Girls' and Boys' Success in High School Science*
> *Comparing Three Ways to Teach Music Sight-Reading in Choral Classes*

In recent years a good deal of debate at professional conferences and in academic journals has involved conflicting opinions about whether qualitative methods are superior to quantitative, or vice versa.

I find such controversies quite unproductive, because the proper issue is not whether one of these types is generally superior to the other. Instead, the issue is whether a given method will yield convincing answers to the research questions being asked. Such a quantitative approach as that of conducting an experiment is hardly suitable for answering the question: "What factors in Lettie Mortensen's life contributed to her success as a school mistress?" Nor is a historical approach appropriate for answering the question: "What opinions do teachers in Arapahoe County Public Schools express about statewide achievement testing?" Hence, neither approach—qualitative or quantitative—is generally superior to the other. Both are valuable, with each best suited to answering particular research questions.

In the following pages, the descriptions of qualitative and quantitative methods and of data-gathering techniques are divided among three chapters. Chapter 4 analyzes five qualitative approaches (*historical, biographical, experience-narrative, ethnographic, activity-analysis*), Chapter 5 concerns three quantitative methods (*survey, correlational, experimental*), and Chapter 6 describes data-collection techniques—*observations, interviews, questionnaires, content analyses,* and *tests.*

The present chapter is divided into six parts. The first part suggests a way to select a research method. The remaining five parts describe the five qualitative methods.

The Process of Selecting a Method

The task of efficiently choosing a method begins with the questions that the research is supposed to answer. For example, here are guide questions for six hypothetical projects.

- In his roles as a social-science teacher and as the Brooksboro Public Schools' first black principal, what were David Johnson's contributions to the schools and the community at large? What personality characteristics enabled him to make those contributions? What philosophical principles guided his efforts?

- What opinions about proper and improper classroom discipline techniques are expressed (a) by parents of students in a high school located in a socioeconomically depressed inner-city neighborhood and (b) by parents of students in an affluent suburban high school? In what ways are the opinions of the two groups of parents similar and different? If there are differences between the two groups, what are the likely reasons for those differences?

- What influences in Marta Garcia's life contributed to her becoming a high school biology teacher and earning the statewide *Teacher of the Year Award*?

- In a middle-school's social-studies classes, three instructional methods used are those of (a) teacher lectures, (b) student small-group study sessions (four or five students per group), and (c) videotapes of social and historical events. What are the advantages and disadvantages of each method?

- What are the thoughts and feelings of elementary-school pupils after an enraged knife-wielding man attacked a second-grade teacher and a custodian in their school? What steps can be taken to reduce the fear and distress that the pupils exhibit? How well do different steps succeed?

- What have been the reactions of seven Chicago teenagers to social discrimination that they believe they have suffered in their classrooms?

With the guide questions for a project in hand, the teacher's next task can be that of adopting criteria for judging which method, or combination of methods, will be most desirable. Three such criteria described in Chapter 2 were labeled *persuasive outcome, cost/benefit ratio,* and *feasibility* (pages 12-16).

Each criterion can be cast as a question.

- *Persuasive outcome:* Which method will likely furnish the most convincing answer to the research question?

- *Cost/benefit ratio:* Which method—or which variation of a general method type—will yield the best answer to the research question, with the least expenditure of time, funds, bother, the researcher's energy, and opposition from reluctant participants and potential critics?

- *Feasibility:* Which method—or which variation of a method type—can be most readily implemented?

A third step in selecting a research method involves generating an array of methods and their variations that could be adopted for answering the research question. As noted earlier, eight general types of methodology described in Chapters 4 and 5 are *historical, biographical, experience-narrative, ethnographic, activity-analysis, survey, correlational,* and *experimental.* Sometimes a suitable method will consist of a combination of two or more of these approaches. For instance, a biography focusing on the life of a highly esteemed kindergarten teacher may include a historical review of her family heritage as well as a survey of the opinions of her former pupils. Likewise, a classroom experiment comparing the effectiveness of two ways of teaching high school geology may be combined with a survey of the professional literature on teaching geology.

The final step in the selection process involves applying the criteria to each potential method in order judge which approach to adopt. This step involves a somewhat imprecise kind of reckoning—a balancing of the three criteria against each other in a way that identifies the one approach most likely to yield a convincing, cost-effective, and feasible answer to the research question.

A Way to Analyze Methods

In the following survey of qualitative approaches, each type is described in a pattern intended to facilitate readers' scanning the methods and comparing their characteristics. That is, each description addresses the same five topics—the method's *definition, purpose, procedure, illustrative studies,* and *advantages/disadvantages.*

Method definition – a typical label and description of the approach

Purpose – the aim of the method and the kinds of research questions for which it can provide answers

Procedure – a typical sequence of steps for implementing the method

Illustrative studies – the titles and brief descriptions of illustrative research projects that employ the method

Advantages and disadvantages – strengths and weaknesses of the method in terms of (a) how effectively it can furnish convincing answers to the research questions, (b) its cost effectiveness, and (c) how convenient it is to use

The methods summarized in the following pages are described under five major headings—histories, biographies, experience narratives, ethnographies, and activity analyses. Sub-varieties under each type are also included. The types are not mutually exclusive but, instead, they often overlap. It is also the case that a given research project may involve more than one method.

Histories

For convenience of discussion, historical accounts can be divided into two major types—descriptive chronicles and interpretive histories.

Descriptive chronicles

Definition: A descriptive chronicle depicts events over a period of years in the life of a group of people (ethnic, religious, regional, social-class, athletic), an institution (school, church, teen club), a type of event (Christmas, Hanukah, homecoming day, parent-teacher conferencing), a social movement (progressive education, back to basics), a teaching method (phonics approach, sight-vocabulary technique, discovery approach in science classes, assertive-discipline strategy), instructional materials or equipment (blackboard, textbook, photographic slides, computers), type of personnel (school psychologist, teacher's aide, vocational counselor), and more.

Purpose: The typical two-part goal of a descriptive chronicle is (a) to record a sequence of events so they will not be lost to posterity and (b) to tell readers what actually took place and how conditions may have changed over time. However, there is no attempt to explain why things happened as they did or to evaluate people in terms of their actions being right or wrong, constructive or destructive.

Procedure: One approach to writing a chronicle consists of the author:

1. Identifying the entity that will be the subject of the chronicle, such as an organization, a type of event, a teaching method, instructional materials, a type of personnel, or the like.
2. Delimiting the time frame to be covered by the chronicle, such as the 20th century, the post-World-War-II period, or 1973-2003.
3. Stating the questions to be answered by the information that will be collected.
4. Identifying the sources of information (people to be interviewed, newspaper archives to search, documents to be analyzed, libraries to visit, books to borrow).
5. Gathering information from those sources as directed by the guide questions, and verifying the accuracy of the information (seeking multiple accounts of each significant event, estimating the motives of the authors of those accounts, resolving discrepancies among accounts).
6. Organizing the collected information by (a) selecting which events will be described and (b) arranging the events in chronological sequence.
7. Writing a final narrative that answers the research questions in an easily understood manner.

Illustrative studies: Two examples of chronicles stimulated by classroom concerns are:

Title: *Spreading the News at Hanfort Prep*
Research questions: How did the journalism classes at Hanfort Preparatory School change from the time of the first two-page bimonthly school newspaper of 1924 to the time of the eight-page biweekly newspaper and five-minute daily in-school television news broadcasts of 2002? Which people contributed significantly to those changes?

Title: *From Horse Shoeing to Computer Repair—A History of Vocational Education in Bannock Center Schools*
Research questions: What vocational-education classes have been taught in the Bannock Center Public Schools since the first secondary school opened

in 1879? When did each type of class begin, how long did that type last, and what were the approximate enrollments in each type at different times over the past century?

Advantages: By compiling events of the past and arranging them in sequence, chronicles preserve information in an organized form. As solely descriptive historical accounts, chronicles are easier to produce and less vulnerable to criticism than are interpretive histories, because chronicles do not require theoretical analyses, estimates of cause, or the evaluation of people and events.

Disadvantages: Historians are at the mercy of record-keepers from the past, because the writer of history obviously must depend on whatever records happen to be available. The danger the historian faces is that those records may be incomplete or distorted. Manuscripts, letters, books, and newspapers can be lost through the carelessness, neglect, or ignorance of people who fail to recognize the potential future importance of such materials. In addition, some significant past events were never cast in written form. Furthermore, the memories of elderly people who participated in past events, and who now serve as a researcher's informants, may be faulty, so that what the informants recall cannot be trusted. Because of these threats to accuracy, a challenge historians face is that of verifying information by (a) seeking multiple accounts of the same event in order to judge the extent of agreement among different sources, (b) estimating the motives and competence of informants, and (c) estimating how the context in which a record was produced likely influenced the form and content of that record. In the past, words may have carried different meanings than they do today. Or influential social conditions that were considered "normal" or "simply understood" and thus required no explanation at the time may be different today—such conditions as ethnic discrimination, differences in styles of life across social classes, differences in men's and women's roles, laws governing people's rights, and the like. Because such factors affect the accuracy of historical sources, researchers are obligated to verify events and their contexts in order to inform readers of the degree of faith to place in the account of events.

In addition to the possibility that a chronicle may distort history, a further potential disadvantage is that readers are often dissatisfied with a mere recounting of events. They prefer, in addition to a descriptive chronology, an author's speculation about what the sequence of events means, that is, why things happened as they did, who was affected by the events, and how event trends may affect the future.

Interpretive histories

Definition: An interpretive history not only traces episodes over a series of years, but it also includes the author's estimate of what the succession of happenings means. The meanings authors assign to their descriptions can be of various sorts. One popular kind is *explanatory,* a proposal about what factors caused events to happen as they did. Another kind is *evaluative,* a judgment about who profited from events and who suffered loss. A third kind assumes the form of *inferred lessons*— generalizations or principles derived from a historical account that can serve as guides to future behavior.

Purpose: As noted above, interpretive histories go beyond a chronicle's compilation and ordering of past events by including a substantial measure of the researcher's beliefs about what the events signify. Researchers vary markedly in the amount and kind of interpretation they offer. Some histories are long on description and short on interpretation. Others are quite the reverse.

Procedure: In deciding what to write about, some authors bring a particular theoretical viewpoint to the history they are compiling. For example, one researcher may select events and interpret them from the viewpoint of *conflict theory* in an attempt to show how the confrontation among different factions determined the kinds of events that occurred. Another researcher may adopt a *great-man* or *great-woman* perspective in an effort of demonstrate how a particular person (state governor, school superintendent, educational philosopher) served as a dominant force in determining how things turned out.

Other authors bring no explicit theoretical vantage point to their work. Instead, they forge their interpretations in an eclectic fashion, offering explanations and evaluations that they intuitively feel make sense of the particular sequence of happenings they have in hand at the time.

The following way to prepare an interpretive history involves a teacher adopting a theory as a guide to deciding which events to select, the manner in which the events are organized, and the meaning assigned to the results. The author:

1. Specifies an area of emphasis for the history as determined by the general research question that the study is supposed to answer—such an area as ability grouping, tracking systems, achievement testing, intelligence testing, corporal punishment, religious education, the evolution of a particular school, or the like.

2. Inspects history books and academic journals in the field of historiography to discover theories on which historians have based their work,

then adopts or creates a theoretical perspective from which to select and organize events related to the chosen area of emphasis.

3. Defines the location (school district, school, classroom) and time period on which the study will focus.

4. States the specific questions to be answered by the historical account, including whatever explanation (estimates of cause of events), evaluation (judgments about the desirability of event outcomes), or inferred lessons that the history will include.

5. Identifies sources of the information needed for answering the specific questions (books and periodicals to inspect, people to interview, documents to analyze).

6. Collects information from the sources and verifies the accuracy of the information (seeks multiple accounts of each significant event, estimates the motives behind different sources of information, and attempts to rationalize discrepancies among accounts).

7. Organizes the obtained information by (a) selecting which events will be included in the history, (b) arranging the events in a sequence that makes sense from the standpoint of the theory, and (c) interpreting the events by proposing what the events mean in terms of the theory.

8. Assesses the usefulness of the theory as a perspective from which to interpret the events, and perhaps suggests ways that the theory could be revised so as to account more adequately for the events. (Collecting data often causes researchers to alter their original theoretical scheme for estimating the causes of events or for evaluating the outcome of events.)

9. Writes the final version of the history.

Illustrative studies: Two interpretative-history projects related to classroom concerns are:

Title: *Staying in Style: A History of Gym Clothes at Baxter High*
Research questions: Since the founding of Baxter High School in 1903, what styles of athletic clothes have students worn for physical-education classes and for interscholastic sports during successive eras? What have been the causes of the periodic style changes? What changes might be expected in the future, and why?

Title: *School Books and Politics*
Research questions: In the Clayton County School District at different times over the past half century, what criteria, principles, or rules have been used for deciding which books should not be permitted in school and classroom libraries? Which community groups or individuals have influ-

enced the choice and application of the criteria? What were those groups' and individuals' stated reasons and likely motives? Which groups or individuals opposed such book-banning, and what were their expressed reasons and likely motives?

Advantages: Not only do interpretive histories help preserve the past, but they also afford the researcher the opportunity to speculate about why things happened as they did, to place credit and blame for events, and to propose how past trends suggest what to expect in the future. That opportunity includes the chance to apply the author's particular notion of proper historiography, to illustrate the application of a theory, or to correct earlier historical accounts that the researcher believes were flawed.

Disadvantages: Like chronicles, interpretive histories are vulnerable to inaccuracies resulting from the questionable authenticity of records from the past. Unlike chronicles, interpretative histories are also open to criticism for the subjective explanations and evaluations that an author proposes. The faults that critics find with historical accounts often concern the meanings and significance authors assign to events rather than the descriptions of the events themselves.

Biographies and Autobiographies

The following discussion concerns two types of biography (descriptive and interpretive) and two types of autobiography (self-written and collaborative).

Biographies—descriptive and interpretive

Definition: A biography is an account of someone else's life rather than one's own. Like chronicles, biographies can be descriptions of incidents in an individual's life without any interpretation of what those incidents mean. Or, like interpretive histories, biographies can include authors' proposals about likely causes of events and about the merit of people's actions. Most biographies involve at least some degree of interpretation.

Purpose: Obviously, a biography is not a catalogue of all episodes in a subject's life. Rather, the account consists of selected events that illustrate one or more themes that the author traces over time. Such themes are usually reflected in the research questions that guide the biographer's work. Here are three examples. The first case features the biographee's educational contributions, events that influenced those contributions, and the subsequent influence of her work. The dominant theme in the second case is the contrast between the two cultures within which a Native American boy was raised. The third case focuses on three themes — the therapeutic techniques that a school psychologist developed over her career, the factors that caused her to adopt such techniques, and the outcomes of her efforts.

Title: *The Creator of the McKenzie Quick-Sketch Method*
Research questions: How and why did Doris McKenzie develop the approach to teaching free-hand drawing that has become known as the Quick-Sketch Method? What experiences in Ms. McKenzie's life contributed to her creating the method? Through what stages did her teaching procedure evolve? What difficulties did she experience in getting her approach accepted by other art teachers? What have her students accomplished?

Title: *The Schooling of Leaping Deer*
Research questions: What were the experiences of a Cheyenne Indian boy, Ralph Ralston (Leaping Deer), when he attended a U.S. Government school on an Indian reservation? What was he taught and how was he treated in the classroom? How did his school experiences differ from those in his traditional tribal culture? How did such a mixed cultural background influence his way of life and his feelings of accomplishment when he reached middle age?

Title: *The Perfect School Psychologist*
Research questions: Over her 30 years as a school psychologist, what techniques did Minda Martinelli develop for helping children and youths succeed in and outside the classroom? How did her early years compare with her later years in terms of her philosophy and methods of working with the young? What were the most important influences on her evolution as a successful psychologist? How were her efforts rewarded over the years?

Procedure: The stages in writing a biography can be much the same as those followed in producing an interpretive history.

Advantages: Biographies are valuable for revealing the unique character of an individual's life — a life which, in its details and pattern of development, is unlike anyone else's. Readers may also derive lessons about life that are inferred from events in a biographical account.

Disadvantages: Like histories, biographies depend for their accuracy on the particular information available to the author. Hence, the view of a biographee's life can be distorted when crucial data are missing or misrepresented. And because interpretive biography involves researchers drawing inferences about the intentions, goals, beliefs, values, and feelings of the people they write about, there is the danger that those inferences may be faulty. When biographers fail to find all of the evidence needed to support their interpretations, they may be censured for being too subjective, for basing their conclusions on incomplete sources, or —out of an ulterior motive—for adopting a biased perspective that results in an account that is unduly favorable to the biographee (too "soft") or unreasonably critical (too "harsh").

There is also the danger of authors over-generalizing their results— using the conclusions they draw from a single life as the basis for generalizing about other people's lives, thereby implying that their biographee's characteristics are typical of an entire group, when, in fact, the person who was studied was unique.

Autobiography—self-written and collaborative

Definition: An autobiography is a person's account of her or his own life. Two kinds of autobiography are the self-written and the collaborative. A self-written autobiography is entirely the work of the person whose life is portrayed. A collaborative study is a cooperative effort between the person whose life is being depicted and a writer responsible for casting the work in a suitable form. Sometimes the collaborator— who serves as the mediator between the autobiographee and the reading audience—is identified in the final publication and sometimes not. Thus, a collaborator may play the role of silent partner or ghost writer. In most cases, the collaborator has been asked to participate in the venture because the person whose life is being portrayed lacks the time, patience, or expertise to produce a well-written tale.

Purpose: A typical aim of an autobiography is to offer readers an insider's view of a life by describing how events are interpreted by the person who lived those events and who is the product of their influence. Therefore, autobiography is intentionally subjective, designed to expose the motives, plans, ambitions, values, joys, fears, disappointments, and sorrows that help explain the author's behavior and fate. Some autobiographies are motivated by individuals seeking to defend themselves against what they regard as unfair or mean-spirited attacks; they hope to "correct the record" or " right the wrongs" they feel they have suffered at the hands of critics.

Procedure: One apparently common approach to self-written biography consists of an author searching through his or her memory and memorabilia to find influential people and key events (critical incidents) that affected the author's life. The writing task involves linking together those incidents to form a chronological chain of causes and effects that account for the autobiographer's life course.

There are several ways that collaborative autobiographies may be created. As one alternative, the collaborator brings to the task a conceptual structure, which consists of a series of questions that define the matters to be presented in the finished product. The autobiographee's role becomes that of providing answers to the questions in the form of mental recollections and letters, diaries, newspaper clippings, and photographs from which the writer can draw information.

Another approach involves the writer intentionally avoiding a preconceived structure that determines what information will be asked of the person whose life is being depicted. Instead, the writer invites the autobiographee to talk or write at great length about her or his life history, describing the incidents and people that come to mind as significant influences. The collaborator then searches through this wealth of raw material for themes, decisions points, and strands of cause-and-effect that characterize such a life. In short, the writer "follows the data" in an attempt to fashion a narrative that traces significant themes and influences in the autobiographee's past.

Illustrative studies: The first of these examples concerns the recollections of a retired teacher. The second reflects the views of a former high-school athlete.

Title: *Teacher of the Year*
Research question: What influences in Marta Garcia's life contributed to her becoming a high school biology teacher and earning the statewide Teacher of the Year Award? Why did she choose teaching as a career? In what ways did her family and her teachers in elementary and secondary school affect her choice and the qualities she brought to her own teaching? What philosophical principles and ideals have guided her teaching career?

Title: *Glory Days—Memories of a High-School Football Star*
Research questions: Upon reaching age 40, what memories does Abdul McFee have of his high-school years when he was selected for three years as a running back on the state-wide all-star football team? What does he regard as the most important things he learned in the classroom and on the football field during those years? What problems did he face as a football star in high school and in later years? How did he cope with those problems? What advice does he have for youths now in high school?

Advantages: The value of an autobiography lies in its depicting an individual's life from the author's own perspective. If the author is candid and insightful, readers are able to learn the individual's motives, goals, beliefs, values, emotional reactions, and interpretations of events that might not be discovered by a biographer.

Disadvantages: The validity of autobiographies is endangered by the fact that they are likely to be unduly self-serving. Authors may take this opportunity to concoct a partially fictional account that portrays them as more influential, wise, adventurous, creative, or self-sacrificing than is deserved.   As a result, the vision that the narrative conveys may, either intentionally or unwittingly, be rather at odds with reality.

Experience Narratives

Definition: An experience narrative is a relatively brief story or description of one or more influential events in a person's life.

In recent decades, individuals' descriptions and interpretations of their experiences have been increasingly accepted as suitable versions of research, particularly by academicians of a postmodern persuasion.   In other words, depictions of personal experiences are seen as contributions to the world's body of knowledge.   It is obvious that biographies and autobiographies, like experience narratives, include a large measure of personal views of life.   However, in the following discussion, an experience narrative focuses on a particular time and on more restricted subject matter than those found in biographies and autobiographies.

Purpose: The aim of experience narratives (or *personal stories*) is to reveal individualistic perceptions of selected life events.   The emphasis is on differences among people in their responses to the episodes of their lives.

Procedure: Some experience narratives are self-composed.   Others are collaborative efforts in which a compiler helps by (a) eliciting information from the person whose experience is the focus of the study and (b) organizing the information in a readily understood form.   The following procedure is one in which a compiler participates.   The series of steps demonstrates one way the collaboration may develop.   The individual whose experiences are the focus of the study is referred to as the *informant*.   The researcher who is compiling the informant's narrative is identified as the *collaborator*.

1. The collaborator explains to the informant the aspect of life experiences that is the focus of interest.   If the informant is an elementary-school pupil, the focus might be the individual's life from the vantage point of (a) the new kid in the class, (b) a talented violinist, (c) a girl on a boys' baseball team, (d) a child whose early years were spent in France, or (e) a blind pupil.   If the informant is a classroom teacher, the narrative might reveal what it's like to teach (a) in a poverty-ridden inner-city high school, (b) students from Latin American immigrant families, (c) beginning reading to children who suffer hearing loss, or (d) high school students of exceptional aptitude in the field of science.

2. The collaborator describes (a) the informant's expected role and why the informant's narrated experiences are valued, and (b) the collaborator's own role (that of recording and organizing the informant's story).

3. The informant speaks freely about the topic as the collaborator records the narration verbatim, preferably through the use of an audio or video recorder so that the account will be accurate. When such equipment is unavailable or when the informant objects to its use, the collaborator must depend on notes written at the time of the conversation or as soon as possible afterwards.

4. Throughout the session, the collaborator may offer prompts that keep the informant on the topic and encourage the informant to elaborate on aspects that have been unclear or inadequately developed. For example, when eliciting a respondent's impressions of being the new kid in class, the collaborator might ask, "What did the other kids say to you?" or "How did the teacher introduce you to the class, and how did you feel about that?"

5. When casting the narrative in final written form, the compiler prefaces the account with a description of:
   5.1 The research topic, that is, the aspect of life featured in the narrative.
   5.2 Who the informant was and why such an informant was a source of interest.
   5.3 The division of labor between the informant and the collaborator in the conduct of the study.
   5.4 The context in which the session took place.
   5.5 Conditions that may have influenced the outcome of the session.

An experience-narrative project can assume a comparative form if more than one person's account is included in the study, thus permitting the likenesses and differences between individuals' experiences to be compared. Under those circumstances, the author may present the informants' stories without adding any analysis, so that the narratives stand on their own and the task of drawing comparisons is left to the reader. Or the author may identify themes that the narratives follow and point out similarities and contrasts among the several accounts.

Illustrative studies: In the first of the following examples, a high-school English teacher recorded a published author's description of how the author approached the writing of a novel. The resulting narrative was then used as discussion material for students in the teacher's creative-writing class. In the second example, similarities and differences among middle-school students in their experiences of social discrimination are revealed in the stories told by seven teenagers.

Title: *Thinking About Writing a Novel*
Research questions: How does the author start in planning to write a novel? What does she think about? How does she choose the setting and characters? How does she create a plot? How long does it take to write a novel? What problems does she face, and how does she solve them? How does she find a publisher?

Title: *Feelings of Discrimination—Seven Teenagers' Stories*
General research question: What are the reactions to social discrimination displayed by seven Chicago teenagers who represent different ethnic, social-class, and religious backgrounds?
Specific questions—What does each of the youths think the term *discrimination* has meant in his or her life? What episodes in each one's life are examples of discrimination? Why did each believe that he or she was being discriminated against? How did the youth feel about those episodes? What did the youth do about the episodes? Did the youth's reactions to the episodes change over time? If so, how and why?

Advantages: As a research method, the experience-narrative approach has been lauded for its ability to discover and "celebrate" the uniqueness of individuals' lives and of reactions to events as described in those individuals' own words.

Disadvantages: An error sometimes committed by either a researcher or readers of narratives is that of accepting a particular person's experiences as typical of some group of people—typical of other redheads, of other immigrant children, of other short boys, or of other pregnant teenagers. This is the error of improperly generalizing beyond the available data. Thus, the experience-narrative approach is not appropriate for providing information about how characteristics of people (honesty, intelligence, beauty, diligence, humility, generosity, feelings of discrimination, reactions to discrimination, and more) are distributed throughout a population.

Ethnographies

Definition: The word *ethnography* identifies the branch of anthropology dedicated to the scientific description of different cultures. Among the host of ways *culture* has been defined by academicians, the one proposed by White (1994, p. 874) will adequately serve our present purpose.

Culture may be defined as behavior peculiar to *Homo sapiens*, together with material objects used as an integral part of this behavior; specifically, culture consists of language, ideas, beliefs, customs, codes, institutions, tools, techniques, works of art, rituals, ceremonies, and so on.

Because one group of people can differ from another in the components of culture that White identifies, one group's culture will differ from another's. The typical way of identifying which group's culture we have in mind is to attach an adjective to the word *culture*, thereby enabling us to distinguish among *French culture, Apache culture, Islamic culture, teenage American culture, the legal-profession culture, radical-feminist culture, nursery-school culture*, and far more.

Purpose: The aim of ethnographic studies is to portray a group's way of life and, as far as possible, to reveal how members of the group perceive themselves and the world they know.

Procedure: When ethnography is adopted as a method for investigating classroom issues, it can take the form of projects focusing on the way of life shared either (a) by everyone who inhabits one or more classrooms (students, teachers, aides, counselors) or (b) by some subgroup of classroom participants (a school's social-studies teachers, a classroom's clique of upper-socioeconomic-level students, or the group of high-school students who work as teachers' aides in the primary grades).

In conducting an ethnographic study, the researcher's relationship to the cultural group can vary from distant to intimate. As an example of a distant relationship, a college student may interview members of a high-school orchestra to discover the musicians' roles and status within their group and also to learn the ambitions, interests, values, joys, and sorrows the members hold in common. Along the distant/intimate scale, a somewhat more intimate relationship involves a researcher joining the cultural group's daily activities as a participant, but still being recognized as an outsider by the group members. Such was the case of a middle-aged journalist, Elinor Burkett, who spent hundreds of hours in a Minnesota high school collecting material for a book titled *Another Planet—A Year in the Life of a Suburban High School* (2001). During the year, she attended

> as many classes, sports practices, play and music rehearsals, faculty meetings, teacher discussions, student bull sessions, and informal gatherings and parties as she could. She became a confidante of students, teachers, and administrators alike, and was permitted to sit in on parent-teacher conferences. She became so well integrated into the scene that at the end of the year the seniors asked her to speak at their graduation and invited her to attend future reunions as an honorary member of their class. (Stossel, 2001)

Still more intimate was the position of James Allen, a university doctoral candidate, who was permitted to enroll part-time in a California high school in order to view classroom-control issues from a high-school student's perspective (Allen, 1982).

The closest first-hand participant-observer relationship occurs when a regular member of the cultural group serves as the researcher. In a study of classroom issues, that member can be the teacher, the teacher's aide, or one of the students.

H. G. Wolcott, as an anthropologist hoping to produce "a generalized description of the life-way of a socially interacting group," has identified the advantages and limitations of being a participant-observer at different points along the distant/close scale.

Ordinarily an outsider to the group being studied, the ethnographer tries hard to know more about the cultural system he or she is studying than any individual who is a natural participant in it, at once advantaged by the outsider's broad and analytical perspective but, by reason of that same detachment, unlikely ever totally to comprehend the insider's point of view. The ethnographer walks a fine line. With too much distance and perspective, one is labeled aloof, remote, insensitive, superficial; with too much familiarity, empathy, and identification, one is suspected of having "gone native." (Wolcott, 1988, pp. 188-189)

How a researcher collects ethnographic data can range between (a) being guided by a precise set of questions or theory and (b) holding no expectations at all about what to observe or how to interpret the observations. Which aim the researcher brings to the task determines to a great extent the data-collection steps to be taken.

At the precise-question or theory end of the scale, viewing a classroom through the lens of a preconceived structure defines exactly what to look for and what to ignore. Such would be the case if we were to study a kindergarten in order to answer the question: Who are the leaders and who are the followers among the kindergarten children, and what characteristics of children and their environment distinguish leaders from followers? Guided by this question, we first define what we mean by *lead* and *follow*, then observe the children's activities throughout the school day to record under what conditions certain children lead while others follow. Or we might start with a social-hierarchy theory that views groups in terms of dominance and submission, thereby focusing our attention on (a) which children are dominant and which are submissive in their interaction, (b) the sorts of situations in which such relationships are most obvious, and (c) the personal characteristics of children that are linked to—and perhaps cause—different kindergarteners' dominant and submissive roles.

In contrast to bringing a theory or precise set of questions to our observations, we could come to the kindergarten to observe everything that happened. We might also lend greater focus to this broad, amorphous intent by trying to view kindergarten life through the eyes of a particular kind of person—a shy girl, a boy who had been much indulged at home before reaching school age, or an ambitious mother anxious to see her child succeed academically. We would then generate our questions out of what we see from this viewpoint. Such an open-minded approach to collecting evidence has sometimes been referred to as *grounded theory*, meaning that the researcher develops a theory out of the observed events rather than bringing a preconceived structure to the observations.

Illustrative studies: Each of the following studies could be conducted at any grade level and in different subject-matter fields.

Title: *Ninth-Graders' Formal and Informal Rituals*

Research questions: In a ninth-grade social-studies classroom, what formal rituals (such as taking roll, pledging allegiance to the nation, collecting homework, starting a lesson, taking tests) are part of the classroom culture? What informal rituals (such as students' ways greeting each other, their personal-grooming habits, attention-getting behavior, amusements, reactions to the teacher) are part of the classroom culture? What functions does each ritual appear to serve? What consequences do individuals experience for failing to observe various rituals? Who applies the consequences or sanctions? What functions do the sanctions appear to serve? How are new rituals created, by whom, and why?

Title: *Authority and Power in a Girls' Volleyball Team*

Research questions: *Authority* is defined as the officially assigned decision-making influence over other people's behavior. *Power* is defined as the actual ability to influence other people's behavior. So, on a girls' high-school volleyball team, who has the authority to make what decisions? How is that authority obtained? Can such authority be delegated to someone other than the original holder? If so, what is the purpose of delegating authority and what is the process of delegating it? Do people who have no official authority wield power? If so, under what conditions do they gain power? Under what circumstances do authority and power come into conflict? How is such conflict resolved?

Advantages: As a research method, ethnography can reveal those characteristics of a group that make the group's culture distinctive, thereby helping readers understand how and why one group—such as one seventh-grade class or one soccer team—differs from another. An ethnographic approach also can expose the internal operations of a classroom or of a subgroup within a classroom by identifying the kinds of individuals who make up the group, revealing the relative influence of different members, tracing routes of communication within the group, showing patterns of friendship among members, suggesting how individuals achieve and maintain their status, and revealing the sanctions imposed to ensure that members abide by group rules.

Disadvantages: To caution readers that an ethnography is not a revelation of the "objective truth" about a group, Denzin (1997, p. 3) has asserted that "Ethnography is that form of inquiry and writing that produces descriptions and accounts about the ways of life of the writer and those written about." Therefore, although authors may contend that they have simply recorded "what really happened," their account is inevitably a landscape filtered through their particular mental lens, so that versions of the same event as produced by different investigators can result in somewhat different pictures. This observation about diverse portrayals of the same group or classroom is considered to be a disadvantage of ethnography by readers who hope to learn "the real truth" about a classroom. However, if a number of researchers conduct independent studies of the same classroom, the diverse reports can be considered advantageous by readers who accept Denzin's proposal that different "truths" result from different people's perceptions of a cultural group.

As noted earlier, the accuracy of an ethnographic report can be imperiled by the relationship of the ethnographer to the group being studied. Participant-observers can become so intimately immersed in a classroom culture that they diminish the objectivity they sought to bring to their research. But if participant-observers fail to engage themselves intimately in the life of the classroom—and therefore fail to understand the language, ambitions, and values of the students or teacher—they are apt to produce a blemished version of what life means to the people who inhabit the classroom.

Finally, generalizations drawn in one ethnographic study can be validly applied to other studies only at considerable risk because of the unique conditions that may determine the fabric of life in each classroom.

Activity Analyses

Definition: In classroom settings, activity analysis consists of a teacher (a) devising a procedure (usually an instructional procedure) that represents a novel perspective and (b) portraying that procedure in terms of its components. Studies conducted in such a way qualify as *research* because they involve "systematically gathering and analyzing evidence appropriate for solving a problem or answering a question whose answer has not been available." The evidence may be in the form of information from the professional literature, a teacher's observations of students' behavior, the inadequacies of a current procedure, or colleagues' suggestions.

Purpose: The intent of activity analysis is to portray innovative teaching or counseling procedures in sufficient detail to enable other teachers to apply the activities in their own classrooms.

Procedures and illustrative studies: The novel perspective offered by an activity analysis may be in the form of an innovative theory, when *theory* is defined as "a proposal about (a) the most important components of an activity and (b) how those components interact." The theory may appear as an analogy—likening one thing to another in an unaccustomed fashion, as illustrated in the first of the following examples titled *Teaching Patriotism as Religion.* Or the innovation may be depicted as a series of steps in performing an activity, as demonstrated in the second example—*Guiding Reluctant Participants.*

Teaching Patriotism as Religion. In this case, the activity involves teaching about patriotism or, more precisely, teaching the characteristics of patriotism.

A high-school social-studies teacher believes that students can gain useful insights into the phenomenon of patriotism if they compare patriotism with religion. Thus, he constructs an analytic scheme that identifies key components of religion that he contends are also typically found in the practice of patriotism. Such components include a hierarchy of authority, holy scriptures, experts who interpret the scriptures, idealized heroes, rituals and ceremonies, holy days, revered objects and symbols, rules of behavior, sanctions for disobeying the rules, and rewards for faithful service. The teacher then applies his analysis to his teaching by creating a unit of study in which students are led to compare patriotism to religion, identifying the religion-like components of patriotism and showing how those components interact to produce events in the life of a nation and in the lives of individual citizens.

Guiding Reluctant Participants—A Fear-Reduction Approach. The activity analyzed in this case is a teacher's attempt to increase diffident students' contributions to classroom discussions and projects.

A middle-school language-arts teacher wished to encourage reluctant students to contribute more often to class discussions. From her observations of reticent students during discussions, she estimated that their unwillingness to participate was due to (a) a lack of knowledge about the subject under discussion, (b) a lack of ability to express themselves clearly, or (c) a fear that they might appear foolish. In her effort to help them cope with the third of these causes (fear of speaking out), she devised the following activity for use at the beginning of a group discussion of a literary work that class members had been reading. The activity is divided into five stages, each supported by a rationale.

Stage 1: *Goal clarification.* The teacher explains that every member of the group should take part in the discussion so that the group can profit from all individuals' ideas. *Rationale:* The extent of participation expected from the students should be made clear at the outset.

Stage 2: *Leader's admission of fear.* The teacher explains that people often hesitate to speak in a group for fear they will appear foolish in the eyes of other group members. She then gives illustrations of situations in which she herself was afraid to speak out. *Rationale.* By using herself as an example, she hopes to show that it's not only common for people to suffer such fear, but it's all right to admit being afraid.

Stage 3: *Others' admission of fear.* The teacher asks group members if they have ever hesitated to participate out of fear, and she invites individuals to describe those occasions. *Rationale.* When many group members describe their own experiences, the universality of such fear becomes apparent. This realization may help diffident students become more willing to engage in discussions.

Stage 4: *Students' proposals.* Each student who has reported a fear experience is asked to tell how that fear could have been eliminated or reduced, that is, how conditions might have been different so the student would have felt comfortable contributing to the discussion. *Rationale.* Students identify causes of their fear and suggest how those causes might be remedied.

Stage 5: *Rules of the game.* Drawing on the suggestions at Step 4, the teacher proposes a set of rules that the present group can adopt so as to encourage all members to participate willingly. For example, one rule might be that no group members should ridicule ideas contributed by other members, even when they disagree with those ideas. *Rationale.* The rules of group behavior are not only made clear, but they draw on the experiences and suggestions of members of the group and therefore may encourage greater compliance because the rules were not simply imposed by an authority.

Advantages: It should be apparent that when a teacher offers a detailed analysis of an activity, the activity can be more easily and more accurately adopted in other classrooms than if it were sketched in only general terms.

Disadvantages: Some teachers who create and successfully use novel instructional methods are not adept at analyzing and describing the components of the activity. In other words, they perform more by intuition than by systematic logic, so they are unable to provide a detailed, comprehensive description of the activity's components. As a result, it is difficult for other teachers to add that activity to their own repertoire of teaching methods.

Planning Guide

To discover a question—or series of questions—that you might like to answer by conducting a research project using a qualitative research method, carry out the following series of steps:

1. State your question or questions.

2. State the criteria you will apply in deciding which of several methods might be the most appropriate in view of the time, expertise, and funds you are willing to dedicate to the project.

3. Describe in some detail the method—or combination of methods—you possibly could use to answer your research question. For instance, imagine that you want to answer the two-part question "What techniques have been used to accommodate for the individual differences in reading ability among first graders, and what have been the strengths and limitations of each technique?" A historical approach could consist of surveying books and articles in the professional literature over past years. Another approach would involve collecting experience narratives from first-grade teachers. A third would require forming a team of graduate students, each of whom would conduct an ethnographic study of a first-grade classroom to discover the teacher's ways of handling the reading-skill differences among children. A fourth approach could be a combination of the historical survey and teachers' experience narratives.

4. Apply your criteria to your potential methods and decide which method will likely be most suitable. Explain the line of reasoning you followed to arrive at your final choice. For example, which of your criteria weighed most heavily in the selection process? And why did you give high priority to that criterion?

5

Research Methods—Quantitative

As noted in Chapter 4, approaches to research referred to as *quantitative* involve techniques that yield results in the form of numbers. In effect, the qualities that are the focus of research are not only described—as in historical and ethnographic studies—but are cast in amounts, such as frequencies, percentages, averages, and the like. An important advantage of quantitative methods is that they provide a more precise picture of the magnitude of a quality than do verbal descriptions. For example, saying that a classroom of fifth-graders learned how to add fractions is not as clear a description as saying that 83 percent of the class accurately solved at least 15 out of 20 problems on an adding-fractions test. Or noting that eighth-grade boys' height influenced their feelings of self-confidence is less precise than reporting a correlation of +.79 between boys' heights and their scores on a paper-pencil personality test titled *Inventory of Self Regard.*

The present chapter concerns three quantitative approaches—surveys, correlational studies, and experiments. The description of each includes its *definition, purpose, illustrative studies, procedure, advantages,* and *disadvantages.*

Surveys

Survey methods involve gathering information about a topic from various sources, then summarizing and interpreting the findings. One way to classify surveys is to locate them under two broad categories—*direct-data types* and *literature-review types.*

Direct-data surveys

Definition: A direct-data survey involves collecting information directly from individuals, groups, or institutions by means of questionnaires, interviews, or observations.

Purposes and illustrative studies: There are various ways to distinguish direct-data surveys. For studying classroom issues, a useful way divides direct-data surveys into five types—*demographic, equipment, performance, practice,* and *opinion.*

A demographic survey assigns people to subgroups based on such identifying characteristics as ethnic background, religious affiliation, socioeconomic status, gender, age, education, nationality, or regional origins. Examples of demographic surveys are projects bearing such titles as:

Trends in the Ethnic Mix in County Elementary Schools
Effects of Religious Affiliation on Moral-Education Programs
Social Class and School Dropouts—A Statewide Survey

Equipment and supply surveys involve collecting data about the amount and quality of educational settings and instructional materials, as reflected in research entitled:

Computer Availability and Frequency of Classroom Use in Monroe School District
The Size and Growth Rate of Morristown's Classroom Libraries
The Quality of Lighting in Rural Classrooms

Performance surveys report how well individuals, groups, or institutions carry out their assignments.

Achievement-Test Results by School, Grade, and Classroom
Teachers' Classroom-Efficiency Ratings and Merit Pay
Ranking the County's High-School Swimming Classes

Surveys frequently focus on kinds of practices by describing and comparing ways instructional functions are carried out.

The Popularity of Phonics Instruction in First-Grade Classrooms
Types of Laboratory Experiences in Physics Classes—A Regional Survey
Teachers' Instructional Uses of the World Wide Web

Opinion surveys involve gathering people's expressed attitudes about classroom activities.

Teachers' Appraisals of the City Schools' Sex-Education Curriculum
Students' Opinions of Their Literature Textbooks
Parents' Attitudes about Homework

Procedure: Direct-data surveys can be conducted in many ways. Here is one example of steps that the survey process can involve.

The survey's focus is defined by the question—or questions—that the research is expected to answer, such as "What do the city's public school teachers believe are desirable and undesirable features of the newly devised drug-education curriculum?" or "How many kindergarten and first-grade classrooms include sight-vocabulary exercises in their reading instruction?"

1. Potential subjects (individuals, groups, or institutions) to be surveyed are identified.
2. Criteria are devised to guide the choice of which subjects from among the potential ones at step 1 will actually be used. The following are examples of such criteria:

   Availability: Which subjects are most readily available?

   Representativeness: Which subjects best represent the range of people that the survey is designed to learn about?

   Willingness: Which subjects are likely most willing to participate in the survey?
3. The criteria are applied to the options in order to arrive at the actual subjects who will be studied.
4. Potential instruments and techniques for collecting survey data (as will be described in Chapter 6) are identified.
5. Criteria for selecting the most appropriate instruments and techniques are established, such as:

   Accuracy: Which techniques will likely yield the most valid answers to the research questions?

   Availability: Which instruments or techniques are most readily obtained or created?

   Ease of Use: Which techniques are the simplest to use?

   Cost: Which techniques require the least expenditure of funds?
6. The criteria are applied to the options from step 4 to select the most suitable data-collection techniques, and the chosen instruments and procedures for data collection are created or adopted.
7. A small sample of the chosen type of subjects (individuals, groups, institutions) that will *not* be used in the final survey is selected for testing the instruments and techniques in a pilot study in order to discover possible weaknesses in the data-collection procedures.
8. The instruments and techniques are tried out on that small sample.
9. The results of the pilot study are analyzed; and the instruments and procedures are revised to correct weaknesses found during the pilot study. If many shortcomings were identified, or if the researcher doubts that the corrections have been sufficient, a second cycle of steps 7-9 may be conducted with a different sample of subjects (who will not participate in the final survey).
10. In most surveys, the entire population of individuals that is being studied does not take part, because studying all of them would be too burdensome. Therefore, only a representative segment (a sample) of that population will be used in the final survey. As step 10, a system for drawing the sample is adopted (as described below), and a decision is reached about exactly which subjects will be asked to participate.

11. The survey procedures are administered to the subjects.
12. The subjects' responses are tabulated and classified.
13. The classified results are interpreted in terms of the researcher's original guide question.
14. A description of the project is written and distributed.

The question of sampling: When researchers draw conclusions from the results of a survey, they either can limit those conclusions to the people or objects they directly studied or can extend the conclusions to a broader population of people or objects that were not studied. For instance, the teacher of a high-school health-education class administers an *Eating Habits Questionnaire* to the 33 students enrolled in her class, then reports the results as representing the self-reported dietary practices of only the members of that class. Her study's results can be labeled *descriptive* conclusions, because she has simply described her students' responses. However, let's imagine that she feels that the pattern of answers she obtained from her 33 students is likely an accurate reflection of answers she would receive if all 2,700 of the high school's students completed the questionnaire. Or, perhaps she thinks that her class's pattern of responses would also result if all of the 13,000 students in the city's five high schools took part in the survey. This application of a study's outcomes to people who did not directly participate is usually referred to as an *inferential* conclusion, because the researcher is inferring that the results from a limited number of participants (the *sample*) are valid indicators of what a broader collection of people (the *population*) would answer. In effect, the *population* is the large group about which the researcher wishes to draw generalizations, and the *sample* is the segment of that large group which is directly studied.

There is clearly a widespread desire among researchers to extend their conclusions beyond the subjects they have surveyed. A political pollster who can accurately predict the outcome of a presidential election on the basis of surveying a sample of 5,000 voters is held in far higher esteem than a pollster who makes no attempt to extend his results beyond the 5,000. And being able to offer convincing statements about 13,000 students' reported eating habits is far more impressive than limiting such statements to 33 respondents. However, it's quite obvious that extending the conclusions about a directly studied group to a larger population entails the risk of error, since the sample may not represent the population in a balanced fashion.

Consequently, when conducting surveys about classroom issues, researchers need to decide how broadly they intend to apply their findings. Are they content to limit their conclusions to the people or objects that were actually surveyed, or do they plan to regard those subjects as a sample of a broader population to which the outcomes could also be validly applied? If the latter is the case, then how can the researcher support the assumption that the studied sample accurately represents the broader population? There are two popular ways to attack this problem. The first involves *formal sampling procedures.* The second involves *estimating patterns of cause.*

Formal sampling procedures: There are numbers of traditional methods of drawing samples, with each method accompanied by strengths and limitations. Four such approaches are *random, multistage, systematic,* and *convenience.*

Simple random sampling. The two most basic rules governing random sampling are that (a) each member of the population should have an equal chance of being chosen and (b) selecting one member should not influence which other members will be chosen. One familiar way to draw a random sample is to begin by defining the characteristics of the population to which generalizations from the survey will be applied. For example, the population can be defined as all high school students in a city's public schools. Or, in a study of school buildings' earthquake resistance, the population can consist of all public and private school buildings in the state. Or, in research on classroom teachers' opinions of a school board's salary offer, the population can include all full-time public-school teachers in the county.

After the population has been delineated, a decision is reached about the size of the sample that will be drawn. Obviously, the larger the sample in comparison to the size of the population, the greater the likelihood that the sample will represent the population in a balanced manner. For instance, in a high-school population of 13,000, having 650 students (5%) fill out questionnaires will likely furnish results that more accurately represent the population than would a sample of 130 students (1%). Next, the name of each individual in the population is written on a slip of paper (with all slips identical in size and texture). The slips are placed in an open container (hat, fishbowl, cardboard box) and stirred around. Then one slip at a time is drawn out until the specified sample size has been reached.

Or, instead of putting slips of paper in a container, another way to draw a random sample is to list all 13,000 students' names and to assign an identification number to each name. Then the researcher obtains a set of random numbers from a statistics book or from a computer program that generates random numbers. The first 650 numbers in the random set are matched against the students' identification numbers to determine which students are to become members of the sample.

The advantage of drawing a random sample is that the researcher can now make a statistical estimate of how accurately the sample represents the population. Various kinds of inferential statistical techniques are described in most statistics textbooks. Those techniques provide an estimate of how closely the results of surveying the sample probably approximate the results that would be obtained if the entire population had been surveyed.

The disadvantage of simple random sampling is that the larger the population, the more trouble it is to carry out the process. For populations that are very large, the task is not merely burdensome but practically impossible. Imagine trying to draw a simple random sample of 1,000 participants from among the mothers all secondary-school students in Texas in order to survey mothers' opinions about whether schools should provide birth-control information to the state's teenagers. Therefore, with large populations, simple random sampling is not practical.

Multistage random sampling. A popular way to simplify the task of drawing a random sample involves dividing the selection process into stages. The researcher begins by identifying a hierarchy of sampling units of different sizes and types. For instance, imagine that we want to study a sample of approximately 500 Michigan high-school seniors' experience with, and their attitudes toward, the use of classroom computers. On the basis of those results, we wish to extend our conclusions so they apply to all Michigan seniors. Therefore, we start by defining a hierarchy of four stages or levels: (1) counties (rural and urban, because we estimate that experiences and attitudes may differ between rural and urban schools), (2) school districts within counties, (3) high schools within districts, and (4) classrooms of seniors within high schools. First, we randomly pick one primarily-rural and one primarily-urban county. Then, within each of those two counties, we randomly pick one school district. Next, within each of the two school districts, we randomly select two high schools. Finally, within each high school we randomly choose five classrooms of seniors (with each classroom averaging 25 students) to compose our sample of 250 rural and 250 urban participants.

This process meets the basic requirements for random sampling (each senior in the state has had a chance to be chosen, and selecting one student has not affected who else will be chosen), and we have much simplified our task of conducting the survey. Variations of multistage sampling are available to accommodate the conditions of different studies and different kinds of populations (Ross, 1985).

Systematic sampling. Within relatively small populations, systematic sampling closely approximates the results that would be obtained with simple random sampling. Imagine that an elementary school teacher, for her master's degree, wishes to write a thesis about how elementary-school pupils would plan to respond to various types of emergency that might occur in their classroom—such emergencies as fire, earthquake, a child being injured or falling ill, a fight among pupils, or the teacher being called away. The teacher intends to obtain her data by interviewing a sample of third-graders and sixth-graders, then drawing conclusions that apply to all third- and sixth-grade pupils in a school district that contains four elementary schools. Rather than interviewing all 2,423 of the district's third-graders and all 2,172 sixth-graders, she plans to solicit the opinions of only 35 pupils at each grade level. To select the 35 participants, the researcher assigns each child a number ranging from 1 to 2,423 in grade three and 1 to 2,172 in grade six. For her third-grade sample, she writes numbers 1 to 69 on a sheet of paper (because there are about 69 thirty-fives in 2,423) and, with her eyes closed, touches a pencil point to the sheet. The point hits number 11. That number defines the first third-grader to be included in the sample. The next choice will be 69 numbers beyond 11 (pupil 80), the third participant will be 69 numbers beyond 80 (149), and so on until all 35 have been chosen. The same procedure will be used for picking the sixth-graders.

Because only chance errors, rather than other sources of bias, are apt to affect how closely the interview results approximate the pattern of responses of the entire population of the school district's third and sixth graders, the statistical techniques (such as *t-test* and *analysis of variance*) found in statistics textbooks can be appropriately used to estimate the accuracy of systematic sampling.

Available sampling. The overwhelming majority of research on classroom issues utilizes what have been called *available, convenience,* or *accidental* samples. Most researchers study the people, institutions, and events that are convenient—ones that happen to be at hand. One teacher studies the way her fourth-graders interpret maps. Another conducts a survey of classroom discipline incidents in a school district's junior high schools. A third interviews parents of high-school students to learn what sorts of vocational preparation parents expect the school to offer their offspring. In each of these cases, the researchers—if they have done their work skillfully—can confidently draw conclusions about the groups they have directly studied. But if they hope to generalize their results to include populations that they have not studied (other fourth-graders, other school districts' junior-high discipline problems, parents of other high school students), they are skating on thin ice. Whereas statistical techniques can be helpful for estimating how well a random or systematic sample represents a population, there are no techniques for estimating how likely a convenience sample reflects the characteristics of some larger collectivity.

Estimating patterns of cause: The best that researchers can do to apply the results from their available sample to some broader population is to (a) estimate what pattern of causal factors is probably responsible for the phenomenon that has been studied (children's map interpretations, junior high discipline problems, parents' expectations for their teenagers' vocational preparation) and (b) to speculate that those same results might also be obtained in a nonstudied population that displayed a pattern of causal factors similar to that of the available sample.

Consider, for instance, the fourth-grade teacher's map-analysis project. She may speculate that three causal factors strongly influenced her pupils' understanding of map symbols and relationships: (a) the children's genetic inheritance (innate intellectual ability and the rate at which that ability matured), (b) the intellectual quality of children's home environments and trips they have taken, and (c) what the children had been taught in school about maps prior to arriving in fourth grade. Therefore, the teacher hypothesizes that children in other fourth grades around the nation or around the world who were like those in her class in terms of her three hypothesized causal variables would probably display the same understanding of maps as that of the children in her own classroom. Hence, when the teacher writes the section of her research report that proposes how her results should be interpreted, she includes (a) her hypothesis about the three causal factors (biological maturation, family environment, school experience), (b) offers evidence and a line of logic to support her hypothesis, and (c) proposes that the outcomes of her study would likely be true for other fourth graders who were similar to her own pupils in terms of the three causal factors. Subsequently, other fourth-grade teachers—whose children appeared to be much like those in the first teacher's class in terms of the three variables—might wish to replicate the research with their own pupils to discover if extending the first teacher's results to other classes seemed warranted.

In like manner, the researchers who carried out the projects on junior-high discipline and on parents' expectations for vocational preparation could also propose factors they believed were strong influences on the outcomes of their projects. And they could suggest that the results of their investigations would likely apply as well to other junior highs and to other parents that displayed a pattern of causal factors similar to the pattern found in the convenience samples.

In summary, applying interpretations drawn from convenience samples can be applied to broader populations only at great risk of error. That risk can be reduced by the researcher proposing a persuasive argument to support the proposition that the main factors causing the results that were found in the available sample also appear in the other groups to which the results might be applied.

Literature-review surveys

Definition: Sometimes the data needed in research on classroom is-sues are not gathered by directly surveying people or institutions but, instead, are gathered by reviewing the literature that bears on the re-search question and by summarizing the findings. A literature-review study is therefore an amalgamation of diverse research reports bearing on a particular question.

Purposes and illustrative studies: Literature reviews can have a vari-ety of aims, including those of (a) synthesizing knowledge, (b) revealing diversity, and (c) illustrating applications.

Synthesizing knowledge. Most research by teachers is restricted in scope, with each study focusing on a specific place, group of people, and time period. However, as noted in our discussion of sampling, many con-sumers of research want to know whether the results or principles de-rived from a specific study might be equally true in other places, among other people, and at other times. In effect, readers often yearn to know how broadly generalizations from a study can be applied and to learn what conditions influence such applications. Thus, the purpose of a lit-erature-review project can be to satisfy such readers' desire by synthe-sizing a variety of specific studies that bear on the same general topic.

The most popular method of producing such a synthesis has involved a researcher (a) delineating the educational domain to be studied, with the domain identified by such expressions as *classroom discipline, reading readiness,* or *computer literacy,* (b) using the chosen expression to direct a search of the literature, (c) identifying themes and trends that are promi-nent in the books and articles that are found, and (d) writing a summary of the outcomes. Obviously, the quality of the resulting synthesis de-pends on both the thoroughness with which the researcher has combed the literature and the researcher's skill at identifying themes common to the reviewed material. However, critics have sometimes found fault with such a method that can depend so heavily on the researcher's intui-tion and biased perspective. Thus, a form of synthesizing that has be-come increasingly popular in recent decades is called *meta-analysis* and is based on the following line of reasoning.

> The traditional process of integrating [the conclusions from] a body of re-search literature is essentially intuitive and the style of reporting narrative. Because the reviewer's methods are often unspecified, it is usually difficult to discern how the original research findings have contributed to the inte-gration. A careful analysis can sometimes reveal that different reviewers use the same research reports in support of contrary conclusions. . . . The most serious problem for reviewers to cope with is the volume of relevant research literature to be integrated. Most reviewers appear to deal with this

by choosing only a subset of the studies. Some take the studies they know most intimately. Others take those they value most highly, usually on the basis of methodological quality. Few, however, give any indication of the means by which they selected studies for review. (McGaw, 1985, p. 3322)

One method of solving these problems of the typical intuitive synthesizing process involves meta-analysis techniques that can produce a quantitative integration of diverse empirical research results. Two of the most popular meta-analytic approaches are those described by Glass, McGaw, and Smith (1981) and by Hunter, Schmidt, and Jackson (1982).

Three examples of projects for which meta-analysis is appropriate are ones entitled:

Typical Characteristics of State-Wide Achievement Testing Programs
Common Features of Physical Education Classes in 12 Middle Schools
Similarities Among High Schools' Teaching Loads

Revealing diversity. Sometimes a literature survey is intended to highlight differences rather than similarities among classroom practices, as suggested in studies bearing such titles as:

Ways of Teaching Morality in Elementary Schools
Contrasts in Policies Governing Student Absences
Variations in Systems for Reporting Students' Progress

Illustrating applications: When a new child-development theory or a new instructional technique or material has been introduced, practitioners often wish to learn the conditions under which the innovation succeeds and the conditions under which it falls short of expectations. To fulfill this wish, a teacher may survey published studies of the particular practice in order to show (a) various ways it has been applied, (b) the kinds of classroom facilities and students involved in those applications, (c) and the innovation's strengths and weaknesses in various types of classrooms.

Why a Self-Discovery Science Approach May or May Not Work with Primary Pupils
Under What Circumstances Is the 'Natural Phonics' Program Appropriate?
High School Biology Field Trips—Why and Why Not?

Procedure: The following steps represent one way to conduct a literature survey with the aid of a computer that provides access to the Internet. The investigator:

1. Identifies the domain to be surveyed by stating the central research question and perhaps subquestions.
2. Chooses key words from the research question, along with synonyms and related terms, to guide the search of the literature.
3. Uses a computer that can access the World Wide Web in order to locate:

3.1 The home page of one or more libraries. From the array of databases that the library lists, the researcher selects one or more that might report relevant studies to include in the survey. For example, the following are potentially useful databases in one university's library holdings: *Magazines & Journal Articles, Newspaper Articles, ERIC (Educational Resources Information Center), Chicano Data Base,* and *PsychInfo.* The investigator opens the selected database and enters each key word in the "search" blank that appears, thereby producing a list of publications related to the key term.

3.2 One or more search engines, such as *Ask Jeeves, Google,* or *Teoma.* When the search-engine home page appears, the investigator enters each key word or phrase in the "SEARCH" space in order to generate the list of websites associated with the word or phrase.

4. Records the results of the search by use of the methods described in Chapter 3 for compiling material derived from the literature.

Correlation Studies

Definition: Correlation research is conducted to reveal how the condition of one variable—such as pupils' levels of intelligence—is related to some other variable—such as pupils' popularity with classmates. In other words, are pupils who score higher on intelligence tests more often chosen as friends than are pupils who score lower?

Or the question of correlation can also be stated another way: What happens to one variable when another variable changes? For instance, when high school students are given more frequent history-class homework, what happens to their history-test scores?

In this discussion of correlation studies, the term *variable* refers to anything that can differ or change in kind or in amount. For example, the variable *gender* is typically divided into two kinds—female and male, or girl and boy. The variable *height* is typically divided into such amounts as feet-and-inches or meters-and-centimeters. Many studies have been conducted to determine the co-relationship between gender and height in order to answer the question: What happens to height when gender changes? Or, in more common parlance, are girls taller than boys, or vice versa? If so, by how much?

Although correlation research most often focuses on two variables, such investigations can also involve more than two. For instance, we could study how children's *height* relates to *gender* at different *age* levels.

The following are a few of the many types of questions that can be answered by the use of correlation analysis.

Are sixth-graders who score high on mathematics tests the most self-confident in social situations while those who score low are the least self-confident?

How do middle-school girls compare with middle-school boys in swimming skill?

What is the relationship between (a) the frequency with which high-school teachers criticize students in class and (b) the frequency of students voluntarily participating in class discussions?

Are teachers who have had more formal education held in greater respect by their students than are teachers with less formal schooling?

Do kindergarteners from one-parent families display more fear in new situations than ones from two-parent families?

Expressing the degree of relationship: The extent of correlation between variables can be expressed verbally, graphically, or statistically.

Here are five typical ways that people verbally describe their impression of the strength of relationship between two variables.

- Students who are good at math are also always good at science.
- Pretty girls usually have more self-confidence than do plain-looking girls.
- I'd say that about half the time the taller kids get more respect from their peers than the shorter kids do.
- Only rarely will teachers give homework on Friday—that is, homework they expect students to complete over the weekend.
- Knowing how fast different teenagers can run is never any help in estimating how well they can sing, because running speed and singing ability are completely independent of each other.

Verbal descriptions have the advantage of being easy to create, and they can also be understood without any technical preparation on the part of the listener. However, verbal descriptions can suffer from two weaknesses. They are generally imprecise and they are typically based on casual observation rather than careful study. Imprecision in the above verbal expressions is reflected in such vague estimates of relationship as *usually, about half the time,* and *rarely.* Although the word *always* in the first example and *never* in the last are precise, such extreme relationships as *always* and *never* are themselves extremely rare or nonexistent in real-life correlations.

It is also the case that judicious listeners may suspect that verbal descriptions are founded on the speaker's casual, inexact impressions or on hearsay evidence rather than on the conscientious study of a broad range of incidents that involve the pair of variables.

Thus, in order to express correlations in a more precise and convincing form, researchers design controlled studies of correlations and express the results in graphic or statistical form. To illustrate how this may be done, let's imagine that we wish to create a written test that enables us to predict the degree of preadolescents' peer sociality. By *sociality* we mean *how adept youths are in interacting with agemates.* We are acquainted with three different theories of social behavior on which a test might be built, but we are not sure which of the three is the most accurate. Therefore, we intend to create three tests, each based on a different theory, and try them out. Each test consists of 36 statements. Pupils are to react to each item by marking one of three answers: (a) I'm very much like this, (b) I am sort of like this, or (c) I'm not like this at all. The typical form of items is shown in these examples:

- Most kids in our class think I'm fun to be with.
- I like to be alone a lot of the time and not bothered by others.
- When they choose up teams, I'm one of the last to be chosen.

Now imagine that our school has hired a psychology student from the nearby college to assist in supervising pupils on the playground, in the lunchroom, and in the halls. We enlist the student's help with our project by assigning him—during the routine of his work—to observe the social behavior of 16 particular sixth-graders over a six-week period and to assess their sociality on an observation-rating schedule that we have developed. The schedule focuses on the kinds of social incidents in which pupils engage and the quality and frequency of their engagement. The observer's ratings of a pupil yield numbers that are summed to produce an overall sociality score.

During the six-week observation period, we administer each of the three sociality tests to all sixth graders. Thus, at the end of the six weeks we have four kinds of numerical information about our 16 pupils—their

Table 5-1

Sixth-Graders' Sociality Scores

Name	Observation Score	Test A Score	Test B Score	Test C Score
Ann	54	33	35	34
Bart	37	26	18	24
Chelsea	12	11	8	13
Darrell	43	19	23	20
Eve	32	22	19	22
Freddie	46	17	31	15
Gwen	27	28	18	28
Harold	19	14	12	15
Ivy	26	18	15	19
Jack	38	16	27	18
Kelly	33	21	28	21
Lance	25	35	16	33
Mavis	46	20	26	21
Ned	35	14	25	15
Oprah	39	23	31	24
Paul	41	20	23	29

scores on the 60-point observation schedule and their scores on the three 36-item tests. That information, along with the fictitious names by which we identify the participants, is shown in Table 5-1. It is very difficult to estimate the relationship between the observation scores and any of the three tests' scores when the data are simply listed as they are in the table. But if we recast the data graphically as a scatter diagram, the nature of the correlations becomes immediately evident. To prepare a scatter diagram, we arrange the test scores on the vertical axis and the observation scores on the horizontal axis. Then we plot the points at which each pupil's score on a test intersects with that pupil's score on the observation schedule. Scatter diagrams for the three tests, in relation to the observations, are displayed in Figures 5-1, 5-2, and 5-3.

Figure 5-1

The Relationship Between Observations and Test A

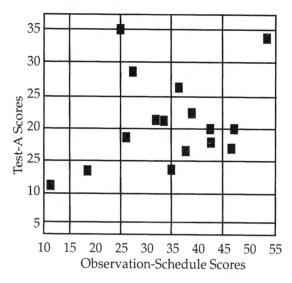

Viewing the three scatter diagrams enables us to judge which test comes closest to measuring the same characteristics as does the observation schedule. We make this judgment by noticing how closely the array of dots assume a straight line extending from the lower-left corner to the upper-right corner of the diagram. If the dots formed a straight diagonal line, it would mean that the students who scored highest on the test also scored highest on the observation schedule and vice versa. But the more the dots spread all over the diagram, the lower the degree of relationship between the test and the observations.

Figure 5-2

The Relationship Between Observations and Test B

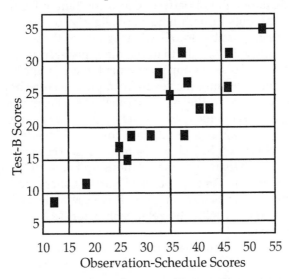

Figure 5-3

The Relationship Between Observations and Test C

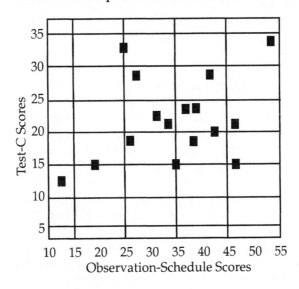

Thus, by inspecting the three diagrams, we recognize that Test B is the one that best predicts students' observation scores, since the dots quite obviously extend from lower left to upper right, although not in a precise line. So, the extent of correlation between Test B and the observation schedule is high, although not perfect. Our inspection of Figures 5-1 and 5-3 shows that the dots in both tend very slightly to spread along the diagonal, but it's impossible to tell whether one of those two patterns represents a greater relationship than the other between test scores and observation scores. To settle our puzzlement, we can apply statistical analysis to the data. Among the several computational techniques that we might use, we choose the most popular one—Pearson's product-moment correlation technique (symbolized by the letter r). Calculating r for the three scatter diagrams results in a correlation coefficient of +.30 for Test A, of +.89 for Test B, and of +.34 for Test C. The closer a correlation comes to +1.0, the stronger the relationship between the two variables. Hence, from the vantage point of our statistics, the correlation between the observation scores and Test B is very high, and it is quite low for Tests A and C, with the relationship for Test C just slightly greater than for Test A.

Therefore, as our examples have illustrated, statistical descriptions of relationships are more precise than graphic displays, whereas graphic displays are typically more precise than verbal descriptions.

Purpose and illustrative studies: Correlation studies are usually conducted for one or more of three reasons: (a) to show how closely changes in one variable are related to changes in another, (b) to permit predictions of one variable by knowing how closely the two variables are related, or (c) to suggest how the condition of one variable has caused the condition of another variable.

An error easily committed by people who interpret correlations is to assume that every described relationship between variables—such as the relation between height and self-confidence—implies that one of the variables is responsible for the other. This is the assumption that demonstrating a degree of relationship between variables inevitably implies that one variable caused the other. The fallacy of this assumption can be illustrated with an anecdote about the relationship between the frequency of storks in Dutch communities and the incidence of births in such places. It was commonly observed that the greater the number of storks nesting in a community, the larger the number of children born there. If we were now to assume that one of these variables (quantity of storks) was the cause of the other variable (quantity of infants), then we have the evidence necessary to support the age-old canard about storks delivering human babies. However, the relationship between the quantity of storks and the quantity of babies in a community is—from both scientific and commonsense viewpoints—no more than coincidental. Thus, a demonstrated degree of relationship between two variables cannot be taken as evidence that one variable's condition caused the other's condition—either entirely or only partially. What is required for demonstrating *cause* is a line of logic demonstrating that a change in one variable was necessary for producing change in the other. In the stork/baby instance, there is a host of evidence suggesting that the cause of the production of human babies has nothing to do with the correlation between the stork population and the newborn-humans population. In effect, it is possible to convincingly argue a causal relationship between (a) the frequency of human parents' copulating (along with information about the current condition of the parents' sperm and ova supplies, and the lack of obstruction to sperms reaching ova) and (b) the frequency of human births. In addition, the stork/human-babies correlation can be explained without any assumption that storks bring babies. For instance, observations of storks in the Netherlands had shown that the birds preferred to nest in quieter, unpolluted villages rather than in bustling, smoky cities. And just by coincidence, villagers produced more infants per family than did city folk. In sum, a demonstrated correlation between variables can be either coincidental (*casual*) or causal. Any proposal that a relationship is causal must be supported by empirical evidence (facts) and a persuasive line of reasoning.

In school settings, demonstrating a likely causal relationship between variables can be particularly valuable in suggesting how teachers might promote students' progress and personal welfare. For instance, a study that included a wide range of fourth-grade classrooms in the United States showed a positive correlation between pupils' reading skills and the number of books in classroom libraries (Postlethwaite & Ross, 1992, pp. 36-37). Thus, it is not difficult to argue that increasing the availability of books in classroom libraries could be one reason for children's improving their reading competence. The correlation and its causal interpretation can then serve as a guide to action, that is, to enlarging classroom library holdings. Furthermore, in the same study, the schools whose pupils were the most competent readers had teachers

> who ensure that their students read a great deal in class, who have their students visit the school library on a regular basis, and who, to a lesser extent, set more reading homework, ask questions about the homework the next day, and devote more time per school week to the teaching and practice of reading. (Postlethwaite & Ross, 1992, pp. 45-46)

However, even when a convincing case cannot be made for a correlation being of a causal variety, that correlation may still be of practical value for predicting an outcome. For example, imagine that we create a *Business Decisions and Attitudes Inventory* composed of 30 items, with each item requiring students to select which among several decisions they would consider the wisest in a business operation. We now administer the inventory to the 98 students in the four sections of our high school's course titled Business Practices. Next, we compute the degree of correlation between (a) students' scores on the inventory and (b) their total scores on classroom assignments (tests, homework, in-class projects). Let's assume that our computation reveals a very strong relationship between students' inventory scores and their total class-progress scores. Students who ranked high on the inventory also ranked high in academic performance, and vice versa. This information suggests that if we know a student's score on the inventory, we can make a pretty good estimate of how well that student will succeed in class work. If we can assume that students' ability to answer the items on the inventory is, to a great extent, the result of knowledge and intellectual ability that they possessed before entering the Business Practices class, then at the beginning of the semester—when students first enter the class—we can administer the inventory and estimate with some confidence how each student will probably succeed in the course.

In summary, when the correlation between two variables is very strong, our knowing an individual's position on one variable equips us to offer a rather accurate guess about the person's position on the other variable. We can do this without needing to assume anything about the causes behind the individual's status on either of the variables.

Procedure: There are numerous statistical ways to calculate the magnitude of the relationship between variables. Each way is designed to suit the particular sort of information that has been gathered in a research project—such as data in the form of test scores, of gender, of age, of answers on a study-habits inventory, of parents' educational levels, and more. Such statistics textbooks as the following describe which correlation methods are appropriate for which kinds of data, what steps to take in calculating the degree of correlation, and the advantages and disadvantages of each method.

Glass, G. V., & Hopkins, K. D. (1996). *Statistical Methods in Education and Psychology* (3rd ed.). Boston: Allyn & Bacon.

Gravetter, F. J. (1988). *Statistics for the Behavioral Sciences.* St. Paul, MN: West.

Hays, W. L. (1994). *Statistics* (5th ed.). Fort Worth, TX: Harcourt Brace.

Jaccard, J., & Becker, M. A. (1990). *Statistics for the Behavioral Sciences* (2nd ed.). Belmont, CA: Wadsworth.

Popham, W. J., & Sirotnkik, K. A. (1992). *Understanding Statistics in Education.* Itasca, IL: Peacock.

Siegel, S., & Castellan, N. J., Jr. (1988). *Nonparametric Statistics for the Behavioral Sciences* (2nd ed.). New York: McGraw-Hill.

Sirkin, R. M. (1995). *Statistics for the Social Sciences*. Thousand Oaks, CA: Sage.

Sprinthall, R. C. (1997). *Basic Statistical Analysis* (5th ed.). Boston, MA: Allyn & Bacon.

Experiments

Definition: Experiments involve applying a treatment to a person or a group, then describing the apparent outcome of the treatment and estimating the reason that such an outcome occurred. Thus, the assumption on which experiments are based is that events are the result of one or more causal variables.

Purpose: The aim of experiments is to discover the causes of happenings by (a) identifying which variables are responsible for an event and (b) measuring how much each variable has contributed to the observed result.

Procedures and illustrative studies: Experimental designs can vary from the extremely simple to the highly complex, with each design accompanied by particular strengths and limitations. The simpler the design, the easier it is to carry out the experiment. The more complex the design, the more adequately the experiment accounts for the variables that influence the outcome and, as a result, the greater the confidence that the researcher can place in conclusions that are drawn from the outcome. This means that ease and feasibility are paid for with insecurity about the conclusions that can be drawn about cause. On the other hand, greater confidence in conclusions is paid for by increased difficulty in conducting the experiment.

Among the numerous available research designs, only three of the most practical ones for classroom research are described below—the *ex-post-facto, pretest-treatment-posttest,* and *multiple-treatments* types.

Ex-post-facto. This is the simplest of the designs, one that fits easily into regular classroom procedures since it involves no alteration of usual teaching procedures. It consists of (a) applying a treatment to an individual student or a group, (b) evaluating the student's or group's performance following the treatment, and (c) estimating how much the treatment contributed to the final performance.

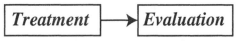

Treatment ⟶ **Evaluation**

This is obviously the typical pattern of teaching-and-evaluating that is routinely practiced in classrooms. But the procedure can also qualify as research if the teacher (a) is seeking to discover the effectiveness of a newly attempted instructional procedure and (b) intends to base future teaching methods on the results of the experiment. The project particularly qualifies as "applied research" if the teacher (c) writes up the findings and circulates them for the edification of other teachers.

To illustrate, a fifth-grade teacher's social studies unit focused on the history and culture of the American Indians who populated the local region before the arrival of European settlers. In pursuit of this objective, she introduced a new class activity—an excursion to the city's natural-history museum so her pupils could view dioramas and artifacts from the past. When the class returned to school, she administered a test covering information the pupils were expected to have learned from viewing the museum exhibits and from hearing the museum guide's description of the events portrayed in the dioramas.

When interpreting the outcome of the excursion, the teacher accepted the pupils' test scores as indicators of how much they had gained from the excursion. However, her research methodology failed to account for how much the pupils may already have known about the topics on the test before they went to the museum. Some pupils may have visited similar museums on earlier occasions. Or they may have read books or seen television programs that included information useful in answering the test questions. Therefore, the teacher could not be confident that pupils' success with the test was an accurate indicator of what they had learned on the field trip, so the problem of pupils' prior knowledge reduced her faith in conclusions she might draw from the test results.

Pretest-treatment-posttest. The next time the fifth-grade teacher planned to assess the value of a new teaching procedure, she could—with a bit of extra work—go a long way toward resolving the problem of the learners' prior knowledge. Before the pupils experienced the new approach (such as the museum excursion), the teacher could prepare a test (pretest) covering the information that pupils would be expected to learn from the trip. The pretest would be taken by the pupils before leaving on the excursion. Then, after their return to school, they would take a similar test—a posttest that focused on the same topics as the pretest but whose items were phrased in a different manner so that children could not answer the posttest questions simply by rote-memorizing pretest answers. In other words, the posttest would an *equivalent form* of the pretest, assessing the same content but with test items worded differently.

When the teacher drew conclusions about the educational success of the field trip, she wouldn't base her conclusions solely on the students' scores on the posttest. Instead, she would subtract each pupil's pretest score from his or her posttest score to find a *change score*, which would be the difference between what the child knew before the trip and what he or she knew after the trip. The change score would be interpreted as showing how much the pupil profited from the trip. Totaling all pupils' change scores and dividing by the number of pupils who took the trip would produce an average of how much the class in general had learned.

This same research design could be extended to provide even more information about the value of the field trip if the teacher added another feature—a test or two administered on later occasions to reveal how well the pupils' learning was retained over time.

Multiple treatments. Whereas the pretest-treatment-posttest design could furnish a fairly trustworthy estimate of how much the children gained from the museum field trip, it wouldn't tell how effective such excursions might be in comparison to other ways the pupils could pursue the same learning objectives—such ways as viewing videotapes or reading a textbook. The following is a design intended to provide the desired comparative information.

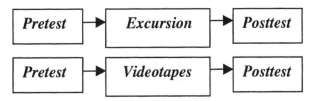

In this case, the teacher begins by administering the pretest to the entire class. She then divides her class of 30 pupils into two groups, assigning half of the pupils to Group A and half to Group B. The intent is to have the two groups be as much alike as possible at the outset of the unit in terms of the pupils' knowledge of Indian culture. One way to form comparable groups would be to assign children to the groups by random means (writing each child's name on a slip of paper, mixing up the slips in a bowel or hat, drawing the slips out one at a time, and alternately assigning them to Group A and to Group B). Another way would be to place children in pairs on the basis of their similarity in qualities that the teacher estimates will contribute to their learning abilities (such qualities as academic aptitude or past experience with museums and videotapes). A third way would be to pair up children on the basis of their similar pretest scores. One child from each matched pair would be assigned to Group A and the other child to Group B.

Next, each group receives one of the two treatments. While members of Group A are on the excursion, members of Group B view the video-tapes. Subsequently, members of both groups take the same posttest, which is an equivalent version of the pretest, focusing on the same objectives as the pretest but with the test items worded differently. To determine which method—excursion or videotapes—was the more effective instructional procedure, the teacher computes change scores for each pupil, sums the change scores, and calculates the average-change-score for each group. The teacher will conclude that the more effective teaching procedure was the one experienced by the pupils in the group that earned the higher average change score. And the greater the difference between Group A's and Group B's change scores, the greater the confidence the teacher can place in her conclusion that the higher change score is an accurate indicator of the superiority of one teaching method over the other—a least with this year's fifth-grade class and with the teacher's particular instructional style.

More on sampling: The remarks about sampling on pages 70-73 apply not only to surveys but also to experiments. If the fifth-grade teacher did, indeed, perform her research project with care (well-constructed tests, well-conducted excursion, well-presented videotapes), she could rather confidently draw conclusions about which of her two teaching methods was the more effective. However, she would be on shaky ground if she proposed that the same results she derived with her class would be true for other teachers in other classrooms. First, we should recognize that when she divided her class of 30 pupils into two groups, each group contained only 15 members. It would require a great leap of faith to suggest that (a) what was learned during an excursion by those particular 15 fifth-graders accurately reflected what children in other elementary schools would learn on a museum trip and (b) what was learned from videotapes by those particular 15 pupils accurately represented what children in other elementary schools would gain from viewing videotapes. Therefore, the best this teacher could probably do—in addressing the issue of how broadly the results of her research should be applied—would be to add a paragraph at the end of her report that said

> In the present study, the technique of having fifth-graders view videotapes about the history and culture of an American-Indian nation proved more effective than did having pupils visit a natural-history museum. But we cannot conclude with any degree of confidence that videotapes would, in general, be superior to excursions for the study of other subject-matter by other pupils in

other elementary-schools. Further research is necessary for settling the question of the comparative value of excursions and videotapes.

The simple research designs described above represent only a few of the forms that experiments can take. Additional designs are available to suit the demands of other research aims and contexts. The nature of various designs, situations for which they are appropriate, and the steps followed in applying them are described in such publications as the following:

Achen, C. H. (1986). *The Statistical Analysis of Quasi-experiments.* Berkeley: University of California Press.

Bonate, P. L. (2000). *Analysis of Pretest-posttest Designs,* Boca Raton, FL: Chapman & Hall.

Boniface, D. R. (1995). *Experiment Design and Statistical Methods for Behavioural and Social Research.* London : Chapman & Hall, 1995.

Campbell, D. T., & Russo, J. (1999). *Social Experimentation.* Thousand Oaks, CA: Sage.

Campbell, D. T., & Stanley, J. C. (1966). *Experimental and Quasi-Experimental Designs for Research.* Chicago: Rand McNally.

Glass, G. V., McGaw, B., & Smith, M. L. (1981). *Meta-analysis in Social Research.* Thousand Oaks, CA: Sage.

Miles, M. B., & Huberman, A. M. (1994). *Qualitative Data Analysis* (2nd ed.). Thousand Oaks, CA: Sage.

Planning Guide

1. Carry out the following series of steps in relation to a question—or a series of questions—that you might like to answer by conducting a research project that uses a quantitative method.

2.1 State your question or questions.

2.2 Describe in some detail the method—or combination of methods— you possibly could use to answer your research question.

2.3 State the criteria you will apply in deciding which of several methods might be the most appropriate. Your criteria might include such considerations as the time, expertise, and funds you are willing to dedicate to the project.

2.4 Apply your criteria to your potential methods and decide which method would likely be most suitable. Explain the line of reasoning you followed to arrive at your final choice. For example, which of your criteria weighed most heavily in the selection process? And why did you give high priority to that criterion?

2. On the line in front of each of the following questions, write the identification letter of the research method that you believe would be most suitable for answering the question. If you believe that a combination of more than one method would be appropriate, then write more than one identification letter on the line.

Research Questions	Research Methods
____ In Martinvale elementary schools, are girls more adept than boys at searching the Internet?	**A.** Direct-data survey **B.** Literature survey **C.** Correlation investigation
____ Over the past two decades, what research methods have been most often used for studying the teaching of beginning reading?	**D.** Ex-post-facto experiment **E.** Single-group pretest-treat-ment-posttest experiment **F.** Two-group pretest-treat-
____ Do high school students learn American history more ade-quately from reading a textbook than from witnessing illustrated lectures?	ment-posttest experiment **G.** Ethnography **H.** Experience narrative **I.** History
____ In what pattern did the city ele-mentary schools' math curriculum evolve over the period 1930-2000?	
____ What percent of classrooms in the county's public schools have access to the World Wide Web?	
____ What rituals in boy-girl relations are reflected in the behavior of students in Elk Grove Middle School?	
____ In Franklin Elementary School, to what extent are families' socioeconomic positions related to pupils' academic success?	
____ In Larkspur School, does students' behavior differ when a teacher's aide is in the classroom from their behavior when no aide is present?	
____ How did different students act during the knifing incident at Morgan High, and how did those actions influence students' subsequent interactions with each other?	

6

Techniques for Gathering Data

Each of the research methods described in Chapters 4 and 5 depends for its information on one or more of five data-collecting techniques—observations, interviews, questionnaires, content analyses, and tests. For example, the substance of a biography may be drawn both from interviews with people who knew the biographee and from the content analysis of letters and newspaper articles about the biographee. A study of sexual harassment in high school classrooms may be based on students' questionnaire responses and on observations of students' classroom behavior. An experiment comparing textbooks with class discussions as devices for altering students' racial attitudes may use both questionnaires and interviews. Conclusions drawn from a science-class experiment about the influence of group-study versus individual-study of botanical terms can be based on achievement-test scores.

The purpose of this chapter is to define the five data-gathering techniques and to suggest effective ways to employ them in teachers' research.

Observations

Observation involves collecting information by seeing and/or hearing events, then recording the results in a form suited to the needs of the research project. The following discussion focuses on three tasks—witnessing events, selecting an observation procedure, and recording what has been observed.

Witnessing events

Observations can be either (a) immediate and direct or (b) postponed and mediated. The immediate/direct variety involves the observer—such as a teacher or a student—witnessing events as they occur. The postponed/mediated variety involves the observer relying on an audio- or video-recording as the mediator of earlier events. Even though recorded episodes are not actually happening at the time the observer sees and hears them, the observer's experience is still much the same as it would be in witnessing events when they originally took place.

The task of deciding what to observe and how to observe it can involve several considerations, including those of (a) focus, (b) intimacy, and (c) the observed subjects' welfare.

Observation focus: The term *focus* refers to the intent or expectation the observer brings to an event. Some people claim to view incidents "with an open mind," "free from bias," and with no anticipation about what they will see, but such claims are self-delusions. Observations are always guided by expectation and intent, as noted in the adage "What you see is what you came looking for." Thus, teachers are best prepared to make accurate observations if they specify ahead of time what they will look for in the events they plan to witness. The most obvious guide to this intent is the question—or set of questions—that the research project is designed to answer. For instance, each of the following questions directs a researcher's attention to particular incidents and selected aspects of those incidents.

What personality characteristics and modes of social-interaction differentiate the most popular from the least popular junior high school girls?

In what variety of activities do kindergarten children voluntarily engage?

How do high school boys and girls react to their basketball coach criticizing their play during practice sessions and during interscholastic games?

During silent-reading period, how much time do different sixth-graders spend actually reading and how much time engaged in other activities? What conditions appear to influence the amount of time pupils spend reading (such conditions as the time of day, the nature of the reading matter, pupils' locations in the classroom, the teacher's activities during silent-reading period, and individual pupils' reading skills)?

It's apparent, however, that during the process of observing an incident, some unexpected happenings that bear on the research question can catch the observer's attention and thereby expand or alter the intention the researcher brought to the event. When relevant but unanticipated features appear in the midst of collecting data, the focus of observations and the kinds information collected need to be changed in midstream. And if the desired alterations are drastic, the data already gathered will likely have to be discarded. For instance, imagine that, in the study of kindergarten children's activity choices, the teacher failed to include environmental variables when she originally planned to view children's free-play activities. But as she begins conducting her observations, she realizes that children's choices are affected by such context variables as (a) the classroom versus the play yard, (b) the weather, and (c) the amount of equipment available (tricycles, doll houses, dress-up clothes, rubber balls). This discovery prompts her to expand her original guide question and, consequently, to increase the kinds things on which she focuses attention.

In what variety of activities do kindergarten children voluntarily engage? How are a child's choices influenced by (a) the child's location (in the classroom versus play yard), (b) weather conditions, and (c) available equipment?

As one way to prepare for such unintended discoveries, observers can conduct a few tryout observation sessions before they begin gathering the information they will be reporting in their study. Changes needed in the focus of attention may thus be revealed during the pilot study before data-collection for the main body of the research begins.

From intimate to remote: The physical and emotional relationship between the observer and the observed can range from very close to very distant.

An example of an intimate physical relationship is a high school biology teacher working alongside three students who are dissecting frogs. A remote physical relationship exists when that same teacher is in the grandstand at a football game in which the three students are players. A relationship intermediate between those two extremes would occur when the teacher sits in the back of the classroom while one of the students gives an oral report in front of the class.

There are advantages and limitations to both intimate and remote relationships. The more distant the connection between observers and the people they view, the less likely the observer's presence will influence the subjects' behavior. In other words, remoteness increases the probability that the participants in an incident will act in their typical fashion. As a result, the observed events will be an accurate sample of the subjects' usual behavior. However, when observers are remote, they are apt to miss subtle aspects of incidents or to misinterpret what occurs. The biology teacher is better prepared to describe what the three students said and did during the frog-dissecting session than he is to describe what they said and did during the oral report or the football game. Hence, the closer the observer is to the observed, the more likely the observer will see and hear inconspicuous but significant features of an episode and will have the knowledge of the context that is required for offering an insightful interpretation of what those features mean.

The emotional relationship between teacher and student can also affect the results of observations. The way students act when they are observed by a teacher who, they feel, likes them can be quite different from the way they act when observed by a teacher who, they feel, dislikes them. Furthermore, the teacher's report of observed events can be colored by the teacher's emotional relationship with the participants in those events. Too much emotional intimacy—too close an emotional identification of the observer with the observed—can damage the objectivity of a research project.

Subjects' welfare: In recent decades, efforts to protect the rights and welfare of people who are the focus of research have led to the introduction of regulations governing how investigators treat people (*human subjects*) who participate in research studies. Such regulations usually appear as federal, state, or local laws or as policies created and enforced by school districts. The general rule governing decisions about human subjects' welfare is that any stress, inconvenience, or harm that might be suffered by the subjects must be far outweighed by the value of the research results—value in terms of the contribution the research makes to the world's knowledge and to the well-being of people, animals, and the environment.

In view of the growing incidence of human-subjects regulations, it is important for teachers to discover, when planning their research, what regulations within their own school system might affect the sorts of observations they would be permitted to make. If a study's results would be reported in a form that permitted readers to discover participating pupils' identities, it is likely that pupils' parents would need to sign an informed-consent document, giving the researcher permission to observe their children and to report the behavior. Frequently, human-subjects regulations require that the names of participants be kept secret. Parental consent might also be required if the research requires changing traditional classroom activities in ways parents might find unacceptable.

Selecting an Observation Procedure

There are numerous ways to conduct observations, with each way designed to reveal a particular pattern of behavior, as illustrated by the following five types.

One-zero sampling: This is a simple method useful for identifying the frequency of a single—or a very few—kinds of behavior and reporting the total number of instances. The observing process consists of a researcher selecting a target behavior, then writing a tally mark on a record sheet each time that behavior appears. The label *one-zero* refers to the behavior either appearing on an occasion (one tally) or not appearing (zero tallies). Target behaviors can include such student acts as (a) wandering about the classroom, (b) interrupting classmates during a group discussion, (c) helping a new class member with assignments, (d) committing grammatical errors while giving an oral report, (e) submitting homework on time, (f) inserting the phrase "you know" when speaking, and (g) putting materials away at the end of art class. Conducting one-zero observations of several students enables the teacher to compare class members in regard to how often they display the target behavior.

Time sampling: During a predetermined time interval (such as a three-minute period or a 10-minute period), the teacher records a particular pupil's every action. For example, a nursery school teacher may observe a child at three five-minute periods during the morning to reveal the sorts of activities in which the child engages as the day progresses.

Multiple-scan sampling: This is an extended form of time sampling in which the observer records all behaviors of one individual in a group for a specified time interval, then does the same for another individual, continuing in this fashion until all members of the group have been observed. The sequence may then be started over with the initial child and continued through another cycle of group members. Such a method is appropriate when time sampling for a single child is inadequate for revealing the behavior setting (since it fails to reflect the group's influence) and when the researcher wants information about a number of children during the same session.

Sampling a selected type of behavior: This method is useful for showing (a) how often a particular kind of action appears in a group, (b) who performs that action, and (c) under what circumstances. Examples of selected behaviors include students'

- offering excuses for their own misconduct
- complimenting classmates
- eating during class
- befriending shy, less popular classmates
- interrupting the person who is speaking
- failing to follow directions about how to complete assignments

Sequence sampling: The purpose of sequence sampling is to reveal the series of actions that comprise a given behavior pattern. The observing begins with the initial act in a behavior episode, such as when a first-grader picks up her book during a free-reading period or when a high school student begins an experiment in the physics laboratory. Recording each subsequent step in the sequence continues until the end of the episode. The results of sequence sampling enable the teacher to compare different pupils' modes of coping with the same kind of problem situation. Or sequence samples can be collected at different times during the school year for a single student for the purpose of tracking changes over time in the student's approach to the task at hand.

Recording Observations

There are numerous ways to record what has been observed. The following methods are likely the most common.

Immediate notes: At the time the observed event is taking place, the researcher can write a running description of what happens. Such a method is particularly suitable when the people whose actions are being observed are not aware of the researcher's presence so that the subjects are not affected by realizing that their behavior is being recorded. An advantage of immediate notes is that they are likely to represent events' details more accurately than will notes made at a later date that depend on the observer's ability to recall precisely what occurred. A disadvantage of immediate notes is that the process of note-taking distracts the observer—at least momentarily—from seeing what is happening at the time. Consequently, important information may be lost.

Postponed notetaking: Often it is either inconvenient or unwise to take notes while an event is in progress, so recording what occurred must be left until a later time. An obvious disadvantage of postponing notetaking is that the longer the interval between an event and the note-taking, the greater the danger that the researcher will have forgotten significant details, the actual sequence of actions, or important participants. Furthermore, the longer the interval, the more likely the researcher will write only a summary of the observed incident—a recalled essence of the episode—rather than a detailed account. Two advantages of postponed note-writing are that (a) the researcher's attention was not distracted by note-taking during the observed event and (b) more care can be taken later in phrasing the record than might be the case when the notes are written while an episode is in progress.

Checklists: When researchers know ahead of time the exact behaviors or contextual features that they want to record, they can prepare lists of behaviors and features of the environment and then, during an event, check the appropriate items on the list as the event advances.

Table 6-1 illustrates one form of checklist designed for recording observations of pupils' classroom behavior. The checklist was used in a research project designed to reveal how effectively pupils' classroom work habits might be improved by requiring pupils periodically to fill out a work-habits checklist and to compare it with the teacher's own list.

Table 6-1

Checklist of Classroom Habits

Pupil's Name_____ Date_____

Directions: Write an **X** in the space at the front of each thing you did today. Leave blank each thing you did not do today.

____ 1. After art period, I cleaned up around my work area and returned art supplies to the cupboard.

____ 2. I handed in completed homework.

____ 3. I raised my hand when I wanted to speak in class discussions.

____ 4. I had my supplies (pencil, paper, books) ready for all lessons.

____ 5. I helped one or more classmates when they needed help.

____ 6. I complimented classmates for their good ideas.

____ 7. I thanked one or more classmates for their help.

____ 8. I laughed at classmates when they made mistakes.

____ 9. I ate food or chewed gum during class time.

____ 10. I threw trash (paper, gum, food) on the classroom floor, in the hall, or on the playground.

____ 11. During class discussion, I interrupted others who were speaking.

Rating scales: Whereas check lists are limited to showing whether a behavior or contextual feature did or did not appear, rating scales go a step further by requiring the researcher to show the frequency or extent of a behavior or some aspect of a context. The example in Figure 6-1 is a scale for rating students' performance in a high-school public-speaking class. The teacher uses this rating instrument to assess class members' skill in giving a formally prepared speech in front of an audience. Each student is rated at three points during the semester—in the first week, at mid-semester, and at the end. The teacher's research project is designed for judging the effectiveness of videotaped-speech analysis as a learning aid. Specifically, each of a student's speech presentations is videotaped. Next, the student and teacher view the tape, and each uses the rating instrument to evaluate the performance. Then they compare their ratings and offer suggestions about how the performance might have been improved. By comparing a student's first performance with the third performance, the teacher hopes to estimate the instructional effectiveness of the videotape-analysis process for improving class members' public speaking.

Figure 6-1

Speech Rating Scale

Class: *Public Speaking*   Student _____*Marcía Kelley*_____   Date ___*11/29*___   Rater _*Ruíz*_

Directions: On each of the scales below, write an X at the point on the line that best describes the student's speaking performance. Use the space beneath each scale to write comments that help evaluate the student's speech.

Situation: (check one)
Conversation _____
Report or panel ___X___
Class discussion _____

1. Enunciation

	X		
All words easily understood.	Most words easily understood. A few words unclear.	Some words hard to understand.	Mumbles. Many words incoherent or spoken too softly.	Continually mumbles. Entirely incoherent.

2. Stammering or stuttering

	X			
Smooth flow of speech. No syllables repeated.	Rarely hesitates trying to say words.	Sometimes repeats syllables.	Often stops in attempt to say words. Often repeats syllables.	Constantly hesitates and repeats syllables.

3. Pronunciation

		X		
Pronounces all words correctly.	Mispronounces 1 or 2 words. *"winner" for "winter"*	Mispronounces 3 to 5 words	Mispronounces 6 to 8 words.	Mispronounces 9 or more words.

4. Grammar

	X			
Grammar always up to expected standard.	1 or 2 instances of poor grammar. *"He don't"*	3 to 5 instances of poor grammar.	6 to 8 instances of poor grammar.	9 or more instances of poor grammar.

5. Logical thought sequence

		X		
Talk moves easily from one idea to the next. No important ideas left out or in illogical sequence.	Logic usually can be followed. Rarely omits important elements or mixes sequence of ideas.	Neglects a few ideas needed for grasping the narrative. Sometimes wanders off the topic.	Ideas often in confusing sequence. Often wanders off the topic or wastes time on insignificant details.	Continually begins illogical place. Omits many key ideas. O... the topic much of t... time.

6. Eye-contact with listener or audience

		X		
Always looks at listener or looks from one to another audience member.	Rarely looks away from listeners. May glance momentarily at notes.	Half the time looks at listeners. *Reads from notes*	Occasionally looks at eyes of listeners. Most of the time looks at notes, at floor, ceiling, elsewhere.	Never looks directl... at listeners. Reads from notes or looks around the room.

7. Mannerisms and gestures

	X			
Gestures emphasize speech nicely. No distracting mannerisms.	Rarely hand, body, or face movements distract from speech. Some suitable gestures. *Fingers bracelet*	Occasionally hand, face, body movements draw attention away from speech.	Often hand, face, body movements draw attention away from the content of the speech.	Hands play with objects. Awkward posture. Face mov... ments distract.

Like written notes, rating scales can be filled out either during the observed episode itself or at some later time. Rating scales place greater demands on the observer's decision-making skill than do checklists, because rating scales require judgments of the magnitude or quality of a behavior rather than merely that the behavior occurred.

Interaction diagrams: A social-interaction diagram can serve as a useful recording instrument for teachers whose research focuses on group dynamics—on how members of a class, athletic team, or club act toward each other. Figure 6-2 illustrates one type of interaction diagram designed to show the direction and amount of oral contributions by six middle-school students as they plan a dramatic presentation for their English class featuring incidents in the life of Mark Twain. The observer (teacher) makes one tally mark for each oral contribution by a group member.

Figure 6-2

Group-Work Interaction Diagram

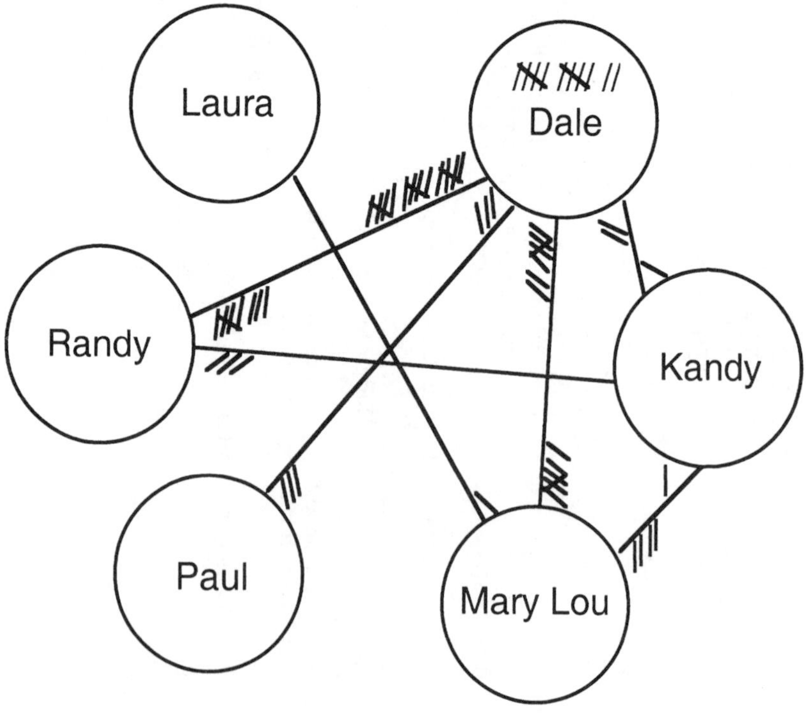

Tally marks inside a circle indicate that the participant spoke to the group in general. In Figure 6-2, Dale, the group leader, spoke to the group in general 12 times. No one else offered general remarks. Tally marks along a line indicate that the participant closest to the tally marks spoke to the person at the other end of that line. For example, Mary Lou spoke four times to Kandy, and Kandy answered Mary Lou once. The greatest amount of interaction occurred between Dale and Randy, while the second greatest amount was between Dale and Mary Lou. Laura did not actively participate at all in the discussion.

Audiorecording, videorecording. At an increasing rate, researchers collect observations through the use of audio tape recorders and video cameras (camcorders). A great advantage of recorded observations is that they enable the researcher to hear or view events multiple times, thereby fostering more consistent and accurate conclusions about exactly what occurred. Recordings also permit more than one observer to witness an incident from the same perspective and thus enable observers to compare the conclusions they draw about the depicted episodes. Audio- and video-taped incidents are typically used in conjunction with other recording techniques, such as written notes, checklists, and rating scales. For example, notes that a teacher takes to summarize observations can be based on multiple viewings of a video-recorded event, or conversations captured on an audiotape can provide the material for filling out a rating scale.

The technique of audio- and video-recording is best suited for gathering information about episodes of relatively short duration, ones that extend from a few minutes to an hour or two. In classroom research, it is usually impractical to try recording events that extend over several hours or over an entire school day.

Interviews

Interviews involve a researcher gathering information by talking directly with people—face-to-face, over the telephone, or via the Internet. The following discussion focuses on alternative interview strategies, advantages of interviews, and guidelines for the conduct of interviews.

Interview strategies

Teachers with little experience planning interviews are often prone to devise their interview questions in a haphazard fashion, when they would have greater success if they designed their questions to fit an intentional strategy. The nature of different strategies can be illustrated with four types that bear the labels *loose, tight, converging,* and *response-guided* (Thomas, 1998, pp. 129-136).

Loose question strategy: The dual intent of a loose-question approach is to reveal (a) varied ways that different respondents interpret a broad, general question and (b) sorts of information that the researcher had not expected but which are of value. Consider, for instance, classroom research conducted to answer this question:

> What diverse meanings do students attach to words commonly used in teaching world history, and what implications does such diversity hold for the accuracy of students comprehending historical events?

Because the research purpose is to show the variability among students' interpretations of terms, the interviewer plans to pose questions in a very general form, thereby encouraging students unrestricted freedom to tell the meaning they attach to a particular expression.

> What does the word *society* mean to you?
> When you come across the word *culture* in the history book, what does that mean?
> If you were asked what the word *oriental* means, what would you say?

Sometimes an interviewer is not interested in the definition students associate with a term but, rather, is interested in the diversity of students' value judgments—their appraisal of people, events, policies, or practices.

> What is your opinion of George Washington?
> What do you think about Americans having the right to own guns?

When adopting a loose-question approach, interviewers resist respondents' requests to have questions rephrased in greater detail because the intent of a loose strategy is to encourage a wide range of answers.

Tight question strategy: The aim of a tight or restricted strategy is to discover if respondents know a specific "correct" answer to a question. Two common forms of tight questions are the open-ended and the multiple-choice types.

> *Open-ended:* When you see the letters BCE in a history book, what do those letters mean?
> *Multiple-choice:* When you come across the letters BCE in a history book, which of these meanings do you associate with those letters?
> > Option 1: "Before the Common Era"
> > Option 2: "Before the Christian Epoch"
> > Option 3: "By Charlemagne's Edict"

As in the case of loose questions, the researcher's interest may not be to elicit an answer reflecting respondents' knowledge of facts but an answer reflecting a value judgment about specific people or events, with respondents often asked to include the reasons behind their choices.

Which man do you think was most important for the history of the world —Jesus, Darwin, or Einstein—and why?

Did the American military do the right thing in attacking the Taliban forces in Afghanistan at the end of 2001? If so, why? If not, why not?

Converging question strategy: A converging approach incorporates the advantages of both the loose and tight strategies by the interviewer starting with a broad question designed to reveal what seems uppermost in the respondent's mind in relation to the topic at hand. Then, following the respondent's reply, the interviewer asks one or more multiple-choice questions. The term *converging* refers to a funnel-like approach —broad queries followed by one or more sharply focused questions. For example, imagine that a third-grade teacher is studying pupils' values relating to proper and improper behavior in school. Thus, when she interviews a pupil, she first asks, "What ways of acting in school do you think are really wrong? I mean, what should kids *not* be permitted to do in school?" After hearing the pupil's reply, the teacher tries to elicit additional forbidden acts that are uppermost in the pupil's mind by asking, "Are there any other ways of acting you think are wrong—other things kid's shouldn't do?" When the pupil appears to have exhausted the sorts of undesirable behavior that come to mind, the teacher asks about specific acts that are of particular interest in her research, such as:

Do you think it's okay for kids to chew gum in class?

If pupils feel they need to leave the classroom, should they have to ask the teacher's permission?

When the bell rings at the end of the morning session, should the children be required to wait until the teacher dismisses them before they leave the room?

If you see somebody cheating on a test—such as copying somebody else's answer—should you report it to the teacher?

If you think the teacher has made a mistake—such as giving the wrong date for when a historical event occurred—should you correct the teacher?

Response-guided strategy: Interviews can be similar to a tennis match in which a player's next move depends on where the opponent has just hit the ball. In like manner, the nature of an interviewer's next question can depend on the interviewee's response to the previous question.

In using a response-guided approach, the researcher begins with a prepared question, then spontaneously creates follow-up queries that derive from the interviewee's answer to the opening question. This technique enables the researcher to examine in some detail the respondent's understanding of issues related to the initial question.

Consider, for example, the following exchange between a researcher and a high-school student whose opinions about marijuana-use among teenagers are being sought.

Researcher: I hear that quite a number of students use marijuana rather regularly. Is that your impression?

Student: Well, a lot more drink than use pot.

Researcher: You mean they drink alcohol—beer, wine, whiskey?

Student: Right. A lot do.

Researcher: So, out of 100 students, how many do you think might have one or more drinks in a month?

Student: Oh, I wouldn't know for sure. Maybe 65 or 75.

Researcher: Yes, that is a lot. What about marijuana? How many out of 100 do you think would have used marijuana at least once in a month?

Student: Well, that's hard to say. Maybe 20.

Researcher: To make these estimates, where do you get your information?

Student: Everybody talks about it, and you see it at parties. If you go to many parties, you see a lot of it. That's how I know.

In summary, as the foregoing examples of interviewing styles suggest, it is important for researchers to design their interview techniques to suit the particular aims of the research project at hand.

Advantages of Interviews

Frequently, the same kind of information collected through interviews could be gathered by means of questionnaires that respondents fill out. However, advantages that interviews have over questionnaires make interviewing the preferred data-gathering technique for certain kinds of studies. For instance, an investigator's taking the time and trouble to conduct personal interviews rather than simply distribute questionnaires to a classroom of students can suggest to students that the researcher particularly values their opinions. This display of sincere interest in respondents' views can increase the diligence and care with which participants answer questions. In addition, the interview setting enables a researcher to clarify questions that respondents may find confusing. Interviews also allow respondents to amplify their answers or to digress from the central topic in ways that prove useful for the research. And interviews may help the researcher understand a respondent's motives, mode of reasoning, and emotional reactions in a way not possible with questionnaires.

Interviewing Guidelines

In preparing for interviews, teachers can profit from adopting six planning steps—(a) select an interview style, (b) derive interview questions from the goal of the research project, (c) list the questions in the intended order in which they will be asked, (d) write the introductory explanation that will be offered to the interviewee, (e) test out the interview process on a few individuals who will not be participating in the final set of interviews, and (f) make any revisions in the plan that seem warranted on the basis of the tryout.

The following example illustrates how such a procedure might work in the case of interviews designed to elicit children's opinions about the distinction between reality and fantasy in the books they read. The teacher's research, in this case, has been stimulated by complaints from some parents that sixth-graders who read Harry Potter books were being indoctrinated to believe in demonology. Therefore, the teacher plans to interview sixth-graders to determine how well they have discriminated between *the probable* and *the improbable* in books the class members had read over the previous months.

Interview style: The selected interview strategy is a combination of tight questions and response-guided questions. The tight questions are the researcher's preplanned queries that focus on specific story episodes and characters that interviewees are to judge as being probable or improbable. The response-guided questions are ones the teacher generates spontaneously in reaction to answers pupils give.

Interview questions: Because the purpose of the research is to discover how pupils distinguish between fantasy (the improbable) and reality (the probable), the investigator's preplanned questions concern episodes in stories that involve children being able to make that distinction. The episodes are selected from six of the books class members have read in recent months—*The Wonderful Wizard of Oz, Life in a Space Station, The Adventures of Huckleberry Finn, Mutiny on the Bounty, Harry Potter and the Sorcerer's Stone,* and *The Great One: The Life and Times of Wayne Gretzky.*

The following are examples of preplanned questions:

- You recall the Emerald City of Oz. Is that a place that actually existed at some time, or is it just an imaginary place that the author of the *Wizard of Oz* made up? . . . How do you know?
- Was there really a girl named Dorothy who was swept up in a windstorm and carried to a place called Oz? . . . How do you know?
- Could a mutiny, like the one on the ship Bounty, actually happen? . . . Or was that just in the author's imagination? . . . How do you know?

- Do you think there really was a hockey player named Wayne Gretzky who made a lot of scoring records? Or was Wayne Gretzky just a character that a story-writer made up? . . . How do you know?
- You said that Huckleberry Finn and his adventures were just fiction—all from the imagination of Mark Twain. But could such a boy and such adventures really have happened? Could they have been possible?
- You said that Harry Potter and his adventures were just fiction—all from the imagination of Ms. Rowling. But could such a boy and such adventures really have happened? Could they have been possible?

Sequence of questions: During each interview, the teacher plans to present *probable* and *improbable* types of questions in random order, such as (a) an Oz question, (b) a Bounty question, (c) a Huck Finn question, (d) a Harry Potter question, (e) a space station question, and so forth. The purpose of the random order is to eliminate the chance that a pupil can discover a regular patterning of probable/improbable questions in the course of the interview.

Introduction to interviewees: The teacher writes out the following explanation that she will use for introducing the activity to each pupil who is interviewed.

In the books we've been reading this year, there have been different kinds of stories. Some stories have been about real people and about things that really happened. Other stories have been fantasies, telling about people and events that the author just made up, and those events really couldn't be true. There also were stories that were fiction—ones an author made up—but they told things that really could have happened. So we have three kinds of stories—true ones that happened, fantasies that couldn't have happened, and imaginary stories that actually could have happened.

Now, what I'm doing is collecting the ideas of our class members about which stories we've read this year were about real things, which were about imaginary things that couldn't be true, and which were about imaginary things that were possible and could happen. By the way, this isn't a test. It's just pupils' opinions. So I'll ask you about some of the books we've read this year, and you can give me your ideas about them.

After I've talked with each member of the class, I'll put all of the opinions together and give a report to the class so you can see how your ideas compared with the other students' ideas. Here's the first question.

Pilot testing: The interview plan will be tried out with three of the sixth-graders who not only will be asked to answer the probable/improbable questions but also to tell about anything they find confusing about the interview session. The teacher will also identify any awkward or puzzling aspects of the interview that appear to interfere with her collecting accurate information.

The refined plan: Based on the results of the tryout interviews, the researcher will revise the plan. If no significant changes are needed in the plan, the results from the three tryout interviews will be included with the results from the remaining members of the class. But if significant changes are needed, the tryout interviews will not be included in the final results of the project.

Questionnaires

A questionnaire is a research instrument consisting of a series of questions people answer about their life condition and/or their beliefs.

The expression *life condition* refers to characteristics of people that signify their status in regard to age, gender, place of residence, occupation, education, religious affiliation, ethnic identity, income, and the like. Such information is factual and is often used by a researcher to place people in categories for purposes of comparison. For instance, a researcher may be curious to learn if high-school boys differ from girls in their attitudes about birth control. Thus, in a questionnaire for collecting students' opinions about birth control, an item at the beginning asks for a student's gender and perhaps for the student's religious affiliation.

Beliefs are individuals' convictions as expressed in their opinions about such matters as protecting the environment, proper behavior in school, people's rights and responsibilities, how to raise children, war and peace, laws, art, music, political activities, and far more.

The following discussion focuses on types of questionnaire items, rates of questionnaire returns, advantages and limitations of questionnaires, and guidelines for preparing a questionnaire.

Types of Questionnaire Items

Questionnaires usually consist of one or more of four item types: (a) dual-choice, (b) multiple-choice, (c) short-answer, and (d) essay or narrative.

Dual-choice items: This type offers respondents two options from which to choose—yes-no, agree-disagree, like-dislike, ever-never.

An advantage of dual-choice items is that respondents can usually mark their answers quickly. Therefore, the researcher can include numerous items that can be completed in a brief time. Thus, for each of the following statements, students are to circle either *agree* or *disagree* in order to show whether or not they concur with the statement.

In the high-school's athletic program, the same amount of money should be spent on girls' teams as is spent on boys' teams. *Agree   Disagree*

Boys should be required to take at least one home-economics class and girls required to take at least one industrial-arts class. *Agree   Disagree*

Multiple-choice items: Despite the ease with which dual-choice items can be marked, they may fail to accurately reflect people's opinions. In other words, offering only two choices may force participants to make a distinction that does not represent what they actually believe. In such cases, multiple choices can furnish the researcher a truer picture of respondents' views.

The amount of money spent on athletic teams should be:
____More for sports that have larger numbers of participants than for ones with fewer participants.
____More for teams that receive higher amounts of paid admissions to games than for ones that receive lower amounts.
____The same for each sport.
____Greater for sports that require more expensive equipment than for ones that require less expensive equipment.

Another variant of the multiple-choice type allows respondents to select more than one of the displayed options.

Write an **X** on the line in front of each game you have played at least once during the past year.

____Soccer	____Tennis
____Basketball	____Video game
____Volleyball	____Card game

Researchers often like dual-choice or multi-choice items because they yield answers that are easily recorded and summed. In tabulating responses to a four-option multiple-choice item, the researcher merely needs to list the four choices and then place a tally mark after a choice each time that option has been marked on a respondent's questionnaire. The main disadvantage of the multiple-choice form is that none of the choices may accurately represent what some individuals' believe, which means that respondents must either mark a choice that is not truly their own or else must leave the item blank.

Completion and essay items. One way to solve the lack of appropriate choices is to use *completion, fill-in-the-blank,* or *short-answer* types of items. In this event, respondents are entirely free to report their true opinions. However, participants who cannot express themselves well in writing may not be able to phrase their beliefs fluently, so the words they insert may not adequately convey their feelings or attitudes.

On the following line, write the name of the two sports that you most enjoy watching. _____
The name of a game that I really don't like to play is_____.

Whenever a researcher is seeking information about people's beliefs that are rather complex, an essay or long-answer item may be the most appropriate.

> Name a person you admire, and explain why you find that person appealing.
>
> Think back to the time that you were very young, and describe the earliest experience you can recall. How old were you at the time, where were you, and what happened?

However, the task of writing an adequate essay requires time, writing skill, and often a complex thought process that may exceed a participant's ability or patience.

Combination items: Sometimes combining types of items provides the sort of information the researcher needs. For example, a dual-choice type can be combined with a short-answer or essay type to yield information not only about which option a person prefers but also the reason for preferring that option over its opposite.

> Directions: For each of the following sentences, if you agree with the sentence, write the letter **A** on the line in front of the sentence. If you disagree with the sentence, write the letter **D** on the line. Then, in the space under the sentence, explain why you agreed or disagreed.
>
> _____1. In modern times, the people whose ancestors were living in North America before Columbus arrived should not be called "Indians."

Summary: The decision about what kinds of items to include on a questionnaire can be affected by a variety of factors, including (a) the complexity of the information that the questionnaire is expected to provide, (b) the reading and writing skills of those who fill out the questionnaire, (c) the number of items the questionnaire will contain, and (d) the amount of time respondents are willing to dedicate to the questionnaire.

Rates of Return

One vexing problem with questionnaire surveys is that of getting participants to complete questionnaires accurately and return them to the researcher. The return rate in some research projects is as low as 10% or 15%. In others it ranges around 40% or 50%. In the most successful surveys, 85% or 90% of properly filled-out forms are returned. Obviously, the higher the percentage, the greater the likelihood that the survey accurately reflects the opinions of the people being studied. Therefore, it is important to encourage a high rate of return.

The chance that completed forms will be forthcoming is greater if:

- the questionnaire is short—preferably only one or two pages.
- the wording of the questionnaire is easy to understand.
- the method of completing the form is easy.
- the researcher explains the important contribution that the respondents' participation will make to a worthy cause.
- the respondents are gathered in one place and supervised by the researcher during a meeting of a class, team, church group, or club.
- incentives are offered for completing and returning the form—such incentives as a bit of money, a small prize, or a privilege. Sometimes it's sufficient to assure individuals that they will be sent a copy of the final report if they participate in the study.
- a self-addressed, stamped envelop is included for returning mailed questionnaires to the researcher.
- the researcher makes one or more follow-up appeals to those respondents who, during the weeks after they initially received questionnaires, have not yet returned the completed forms.
- the questionnaire is administered as a personal interview during which the researcher fills out the form in keeping with a participant's replies to oral questions.

Questionnaire Advantages and Limitations

Perhaps the greatest strength of questionnaires, when compared to such data-collection methods as interviews and observations, is that they enable a researcher to collect large amounts of information in a short period of time and with relatively little bother. Furthermore, if the questionnaires are sent to respondents through the mail or over the Internet, the researcher can collect data from distant sites without needing to travel; and participants can complete mailed forms at whatever times they find convenient.

However, questionnaire surveys are accompanied by several potential difficulties. Whenever the forms are sent by mail, recipients can neglect to fill them out and return them. In addition, if recipients' reading skills are not sufficient to ensure that they accurately understand the questions, their answers cannot be trusted. And if participants wish to qualify their answers by explaining in detail why the printed options do not adequately reflect the participants' views, such explanations are usually more difficult to offer in writing than to give orally during an interview.

Questionnaire Guidelines

A six-step approach to creating a questionnaire can be illustrated with the example of a survey of discipline methods teachers use with high-school students who violate classroom rules.

Stating the research question: The researcher specifies the main question and its constituent subquestions that the questionnaire responses will be expected to answer.

How do teachers treat the following five kinds of student behavior?
  (a) Failing to hand in a homework assignment
  (b) Cursing or mocking the teacher in front of other students
  (c) Stealing school property or a classmate's possessions
  (d) Cheating on a test
  (e) Chewing gum or eating food in class
What reasons do teachers offer for the actions they recommend for various sorts of student misconduct?

Deciding on the method of administering the questionnaire: Teachers' ways of dealing with infractions of classroom rules could be collected by means of questionnaires (a) distributed during a school's faculty meeting and filled out during the meeting, (b) distributed at a regional or city-wide teachers conference, (c) mailed to teachers, or (d) administered via the Internet. It is useful to make this decision before constructing the questionnaire because the decision can influence the form in which items are cast and the explanation of how to complete the instrument. For instance, in the discipline-techniques survey, the teacher may decide that:

The questionnaires will be distributed at a citywide teachers conference at which the researcher (a) explains the importance of the research and (b) informs teachers that each one who completes and returns the questionnaire will receive a copy of the final report. A self-addressed, stamped envelope for returning the instrument will be included in each questionnaire packet.

Selecting the form that questionnaire items will assume: As noted above, items can be cast in a variety of styles. Which style will be most appropriate depends on such considerations as (a) the reading and writing ability of the questionnaire recipients, (b) the recipients' opinions about the importance of the questionnaire, (c) the complexity of the process of answering items, and (d) the number of items included.

The questionnaire will consist entirely of one type of item—a description of a specific case of a rule infraction, along with a request for the teacher to write what she or he would do in such a case and to explain why that action would be appropriate. There will be eight such items. Here is an example:

"During a classroom math test, the teacher saw a boy attempt to slip a sheet of paper to a friend across the aisle. The teacher stepped forward and intercepted the sheet, which contained answers to several of the test questions."

Planning the sequence in which items will appear: The order in which respondents meet items can influence their answers. For example, if the more difficult-to-answer items are met early in the questionnaire, respondents may become discouraged and fail to complete the instrument. In such cases, it would be better to locate the easier-to-answer items near the beginning so participants could feel confident that the task is doable. However, if multiple-choice questions are placed earlier than open-ended questions (short answer, essay), respondents may take the easy way out by restricting their open-ended answers to options they draw from the previous multiple choices instead of taking the time and thought to create answers that more accurately represent their own beliefs.

In effect, the sequencing of items should be based on the questionnaire creator's estimate of how the order of questions is likely to affect participants' responses.

The eight classroom cases will be offered in a sequence based on the likely frequency of misconduct, with more frequent infractions coming first and the least frequent coming later. The purpose of such a pattern is to confront respondents first with cases that they routinely encounter and therefore already have in mind methods for handling those types. Cases that are less frequent and may require more thought will be met later in the questionnaire.

Writing the directions: The directions for completing the questionnaire should be stated in simple language and may include a specific example of how to answer a particular type of item if that type might be unusual in the respondents' experience.

Directions: In the following paragraphs you will find eight cases of students misbehaving. After you read a case, please (a) write in the space below it what you would do about the misbehavior if you were the teacher in that case, and then (b) explain why you think the actions that you suggest would be appropriate. If you need more space to write, please use the back of the sheet to continue your explanation.

Trying out the questionnaire: Administering the initial version of the instrument to a few respondents—then asking them about difficulties they had completing the instrument—can aid the questionnaire creator in revising the instrument to correct its flaws before it is used with the main group of people who are the focus of the research.

Six junior-high-school teachers will be asked to take the original version of the questionnaire. They are asked to complete the questionnaire and then, in an interview with the researcher, to explain any confusion or difficulty they experienced with the directions, the wording of items, the nature of the misbehaviors in the cases, the length of the questionnaire, and other matters that caused them concern. Junior-high-school teachers will be used in the tryout so that the tryout will not diminish the size of the group of high-school teachers who will be asked to participate in the final questionnaire survey.

After the questionnaire has been cast in its final version, its author needs to (a) identify the kinds teachers to whom the questionnaire will be offered, (b) decide on what incentives, if any, can be provided to participants in order to elicit a high percentage of returned questionnaires, (c) compose a letter that introduces the questionnaire study to the participating teachers, and (d) be ready to send a follow-up request to teachers who have not returned completed questionnaires to the author within several weeks after the initial request was sent out.

Content Analyses

Conducting content analysis involves searching through communications to answer research questions. Traditionally, the communications subjected to analysis have been written or printed documents—letters, memoirs, published speeches, scholarly journals, newspaper articles, books, and the like. However, in more recent times, a variety of other media have also become the object of analysis—audio recordings, still photographs, motion pictures, video recordings, dramatic performances, and more.

The following discussion focuses on types of analysis and typical steps in examining a communication.

Types of Analysis

Three common sorts of analysis are ones that focus on qualitative, quantitative, or patterning characteristics of a communication. Conducting qualitative analysis involves answering the question: What *kinds* of things does the communication include? Quantitative analysis is directed by the question: What *amounts* of things does the communication contain? Patterning or organizational analysis concerns the question: What *relationships* does the communication describe among things? Analyses sometimes involve two or all three of these types.

Qualitative and quantitative analyses: The distinction between qualitative and quantitative searches is illustrated in Table 6-2 in the form of questions that content analyses are intended to answer. The first example requires the inspection of students' written assignments, the second uses reading textbooks, the third employs police records, and the fourth focuses on a newspaper's letters-to-the-editor.

Table 6-2

Qualitative and Quantitative Content Analysis

Qualitative Type	*Quantitative Type*
What kinds of errors do Washington Middle School students make in their written work?	Which words do Washington Middle School students most frequently misspell in their written work?
What character traits are described or implied for females as compared to males in the reading books used in grades 1 through 6?	In the reading books used in grades 1 through 6, how often are particular character traits identified with males and how often with females?
In police reports about illicit drugs used by teenagers, what different drugs are identified?	In police reports, what is the incidence of the use of each identified drug by teenagers at different age levels?
Among letters to the editor of the local newspaper over a two-month period, what variety of reasons were offered by letter writers in support of, or in objection to, the proposal that each junior high adopt a uniform as students' required style of dress at school?	Among letters to the editor of the local newspaper over a two-month period, how many letter writers favored the uniforms proposal and how many opposed it?

Patterning or organizational analysis: The purpose of patterning analysis is to reveal the way the components of events or organizations interact to produce an outcome of interest to the researcher. Ways of distinguishing between simple qualitative analysis (identifying the kinds of things that participate in events) and patterning analysis (identifying the ways things are related to each other) are suggested by the examples in Table 6-3.

Table 6-3

Qualitative and Patterning Content Analysis

Qualitative Type	*Patterning Type*
In the autobiography titled *Fifty Years in a Country School,* who were the people the author credits with affecting her life?	By what means did the people mentioned in *Fifty Years in a Country School* affect the author's life, and how did she influence their lives?

As described in newspaper reports, what groups and individuals were active supporters of banning *Huckleberry Finn* and *Catcher in the Rye* from the school district's classrooms and libraries, and what groups and individuals opposed the ban?

According to board-of-education-meetings minutes and newspaper reports, what sequence of events in the book-banning conflict took place over the four-month period? That is, how did the ban's supporters and opponents act in response to each other's actions?

In the audio recordings of the six meetings at which community members offered suggestions to the district's curriculum-development committee about the proposed content changes in the elementary-schools' social-studies program,

which ethnic and religious groups were represented by the people who spoke, and what were each group's suggestions?

what coalitions among ethnic and religious groups were reflected in the remarks offered by their representatives, and how did the form of coalitions and their proposals change over the course of the six meetings?

Steps in Conducting Content Analyses

One approach to analyzing a communication consists of seven steps, as demonstrated in the following study of successful ways to accommodate pupils with hearing impairments in regular primary-grade classrooms (kindergarten through grade 3).

Stating the research question: The main research question and its constituent subquestions that will guide the analysis are specified.

What techniques can be used to integrate pupils with hearing impairments into mainstream primary-grade classrooms, and under what conditions does each technique best succeed?

How is a child's hearing impairment assessed?

In what ways do different degrees of hearing loss affect pupils' successful participation in the different types of primary-grade learning activities?

What techniques have been used to aid hearing-impaired children with the various primary-grade learning activities?

What characteristics of the hearing-impaired child, the school's facilities, the other pupils, the teacher, special services, and parents influence the effectiveness of different instructional techniques?

How can the effectiveness of instructional techniques be evaluated?

Identifying pertinent communications: The kinds of communications that will likely provide answers to the search questions are suggested.

Potentially valuable published sources bearing on special education—and particularly on pupils' hearing problems—include (a) books, (b) academic journals, (c) conference and workshop proceedings, (d) magazines for teachers, (e) instructional manuals that accompany primary-grade textbooks, and (f) the World Wide Web.

Locating sources of communications: The researcher estimates where the relevant communications will be found, and copies of the selected resources are obtained so their contents can be analyzed.

Books, journals, and conference proceedings can be found in university libraries and, to a limited extent, in public libraries. Instructional manuals that accompany textbooks are often available in (a) the curriculum-materials section of university libraries, (b) teaching-resources collections in elementary schools, and (c) school districts' central curriculum offices. World Wide Web sites are accessed via the computer Internet.

Devising a search strategy: A method is adopted for efficiently examining the communications' contents.

Step 1: Create a list of key words to guide (a) the choice of books, journals, conference proceedings, and World Wide Web sites and (b) the search for materials within books, journals, proceedings, instructors' manuals, and web sites. Potentially useful key words include: *hearing disorders, hard of hearing, impaired hearing, hearing impairment, defective hearing, auditory disorders, auditory defects, deafness.*

Step 2: Visit libraries to obtain books, journals, and proceedings.
Visit school or school-district curriculum-resource locations to obtain instructors' manuals and lesson plans.
Use a computer that has Internet access to locate relevant websites.

Step 3: Search the obtained resources in the following manner.
—Books: Inspect the table of contents and index for key words. Examine a book's pages that have been located by means of the table of contents and index. Take notes or make photocopies of material that helps answer the research questions.
—Journals, proceedings: Inspect academic journals and conference proceedings (collections of research papers given at conferences of professional associations or academic societies). Skim the tables of contents for relevant articles. Each article in a journal or proceedings is often prefaced by an abstract that summarizes the essence of the article; the abstract may suggest whether it will be worthwhile to read the entire article.
—Instructional manuals, lesson plans: The guidebooks that accompany school textbooks frequently contain lesson plans that can be skimmed for pertinent material. Furthermore, teachers' manuals issued by the curriculum-development division of school districts or state departments of education may propose teaching methods suitable for learners with impairments.

—The World Wide Web: Use a computer to reach the Internet. Open a browser (such as Explorer or Netscape) and select a search engine (such as Google, Altavista, or Teoma). In the engine's "search" blank, enter a key word. Inspect the extensive list of websites that is thus generated, and open any that appear to contain the desired sorts of information. With the computer's "copy" function, extract any passages that seem useful and insert the passages into a file created for such material. Also, make a note of the web address, which will be needed if the material is cited in the final research report.

Applying the strategy: The search method is put into practice and revised on the basis of practical experience.

The process of searching for information can produce additional key words and sources of teaching practices that can usefully be adopted.

Recording the findings: An efficient way of recording the search results is established.

The principal ways of recording search results are:
—Taking handwritten notes that later are typed into computer files bearing labels identifying the principal research questions—such labels as *assessing hearing, children's learning difficulties, teaching techniques, school facilities,* and *evaluating instructional effectiveness;*
—Typing notes directly into the computer files; and
—Photocopying segments of source materials.

Summarizing and interpreting the results: The collection of findings is reviewed, generalizations are drawn, and the significance that the results bear for answering the original research question is proposed.

Tests

As both teachers and students well know, tests are assessment instruments that pose problems for students to solve. By far the most popular type of test is the paper/pencil variety—a printed set of questions that test-takers are to answer either by choosing a correct response from among several options (multiple-choice or matching items) or by writing a response (fill-in, short-answer, essay items). With the invention of the personal computer, tests have increasingly been administered on computers rather than in paper form. A less common type of test is the oral quiz that involves a tester questioning one student at a time, with the student expected to respond orally. A third type is the observed-performance kind in which the student is assigned a task to execute—drive a car, prepare a meal, run a mile, operate a computer, do a dance, assemble a puzzle.

Which of these types will be most appropriate for a given research project depends on such conditions as (a) the sort of knowledge or skills the researcher is studying, (b) the age levels of the individuals who are to be tested, (c) the number of individuals to test, (d) the amount of time the researcher can spend testing, and (d) the availability of test materials, testing sites, and student participants.

The following discussion focuses on three features of tests that are important for teachers to recognize when they consider using tests in their research: (a) test domains and uses, (b) test qualities, and (c) steps in creating achievement tests.

Test Domains and Uses

The expression *test domains* refers to the aspects of students' personalities, knowledge, or skills that a test is supposed to evaluate. Each test is designed to assess individuals' status in a particular domain. Here are some examples of domains: emotional stability, self-confidence, general intelligence, reading comprehension, knowledge of American history, knowledge of genetic theory, recall of Spanish-language grammar, computer-keyboarding speed, musical tonal memory, visual acuity, arm strength, accuracy in solving algebraic equations, and hundreds more.

The term *test uses* refers to how the researcher intends to interpret and apply the test results. The use that will be made of test results is often implied in the test's title. An *achievement* test is used to determine how well students have mastered their study of a particular domain—mathematics, spelling, Greek history, auto-engine repair, computer programming, clothing design, and such. The results of achievement tests may be used to assign students grades, to determine if students deserve to be promoted to a higher grade or graduated from a program, and to inform colleges and potential employers of the level of students' performance in various domains. An *intelligence* or *aptitude* test is used to predict how well a student is likely to accomplish some future task, such as learning job skills or succeeding in a college academic program. A *personality* test is intended to reveal the underlying sources of individuals' interests, motives, and ways of coping with events in their lives. Personality tests are used by counselors and therapists for helping students achieve more constructive control of their behavior and improve their personal-social adjustment.

As teachers plan their research projects, they can profit from deciding (a) whether a test will be appropriate for collecting the data they need, (b) which domain should be the focus of the test, (c) whether a suitable test is already available, and (d) how they intend to use the test results.

Test Qualities

Teachers have four main options for obtaining a suitable test for their research project: (a) use an existing test, (b) revise an existing test, (c) create a new test, or (d) assign someone else to create a test.

The question of whether a proper test is already available brings up the issue of what characteristics render a test appropriate for the teacher's project. Three characteristics that warrant attention are *reliability*, *validity*, and *suitability*.

Reliability: The word *reliability* refers to a test's consistency. Two types of consistency are *test-retest reliability* and *alternate-forms reliability*.

With the test-retest type, the question addressed is: How consistently do students answer the test questions one day in the same way they answered them on an earlier day? To measure test-retest reliability, the same test is administered to a group of students on two occasions that are a few days or perhaps a week or so apart. Then the pattern of each student's answers from the first occasion are compared with the pattern from the second occasion, and the extent of consistency is reported. The task of making the comparison usually consists of computing the degree of correlation between students' scores from the first and second testings. Thus, a history test administered on two occasions—two weeks apart—to 50 high-school juniors may yield a correlation coefficient of +.91, which suggests that each student's score on the first day was nearly the same as on the second day. The test is thus judged to be a highly consistent measure of the students' knowledge of the history topics the test was designed to appraise. In contrast, a coefficient of +.67—or even worse, +.38—suggests that the test cannot be trusted to evaluate students' knowledge consistently, so the instrument should be revised or discarded. Frequently the reason for low test-retest reliability is that test items are worded badly or the directions for answering the test are confusing, so students end up guessing the answers, with their guesses differing from one day to the next. Low test-retest correlations can also result if a long period (such as several months) separates the two testing sessions. During that period, some students may have learned additional history, enabling them to succeed better on the second occasion than on the first.

In alternate-forms reliability, the question is: How consistently do students' patterns of answers on one version of a test match the pattern on another—supposedly equivalent—version of that same test? Experimental research on teaching methods often requires that students be tested both before and after experiencing a particular instructional method so as to determine how much they learned from the experience. Using exactly the same test for both the pretesting and posttesting entails the risk of students simply remembering items from the pretesting when they take the posttest, so what they learned during the instructional period is not accurately measured. Therefore, it is useful to have two equivalent forms of the same test, with one form serving as the pretest and the other as the posttest. The material measured by both tests is identical, but the wording and sequence of items on one form is different than on the other form. The usual method for determining the extent to which the alternate forms are equal involves having students take both forms on the same occasion, or perhaps one day apart, and then computing the correlation between students' scores on the two forms. A correlation coefficient of +.86 or +.90 in a comparison of two reading-comprehension tests indicates that the two versions are nearly equivalent as measures of reading ability. Far less faith could be placed in the tests being highly similar if the coefficient is +.58 or +.47.

In summary, it is important that tests consistently measure whatever it is that they are designed to assess. When teachers search for a published test to use in their research, they can profitably inspect the technical information in the manual that accompanies the test in order to learn the type and magnitude of the test's reliability.

Validity: The question to ask about validity is: How well does the test measure what it's supposed to measure?

There are various types of validity. For example, the term *predictive validity* refers to how well a test foretells how a student will succeed in a specified endeavor, so a test's predictive validity is determined by comparing students' test scores with their performance in the particular endeavor. The words *aptitude, intelligence,* or *ability* often appear in a test's title to suggest that the test indicates how well students succeed in the realm identified in the test title—*college aptitude, social intelligence, science ability,* or the like. The usual way of estimating a test's predictive validity consists of (a) administering the test to a group of students, (b) sometime later evaluating their success in the selected endeavor (college grades, grades in science classes, observed social relations), and (c) calculating the correlation between students' test scores and their rank in the selected endeavor.

Another type of validity of particular importance to teachers is *content validity:* How faithfully does the test sample students' knowledge and skills in the subject-matter field that is the intended focus of the test? The question concerns *achievement tests,* whose content validity is determined by comparing the content of the test items with the content of the curriculum (course of study, students' textbook, teacher's lesson plans) in the field of interest. The expression *subject-matter field* refers to the realm of material that the test is expected to cover. The more precisely the field is delimited, the easier it is for the researcher to estimate a test's content validity. Here are examples of ways fields may be defined.

Adding, subtracting, multiplying, and dividing decimal fractions

The historical facts and theories in Chapter 7 of the high school textbook: *American Pageant—1750-1900*

The musical terminology taught during the three-week unit on music reading and theory

All rules in the *Soccer Rules Guidebook*

All spelling words on the lists for the first semester

The fuel-system diagnostic techniques in booklet number six

The task of conducting this comparison involves going through the test, item by item, and matching the items to the field's content, with the comparison guided by such questions as:

Are there test items focusing on each major type of knowledge or skill in the subject-matter field?

Are there more items—or at least more demanding items—focusing on the most important content areas of the subject-matter field?

Have the students had a fair chance to acquire the knowledge and skills that the test items sample?

The last of these questions is particularly important to ask about published achievement tests, such as the ones used in statewide or nationwide achievement-testing programs. Frequently there are items in those tests calling for knowledge or skills that students in a specific school or class have never studied. Hence, such items are not valid measures of how well students have learned what they were taught.

In summary, the degree of content validity of an achievement test depends on (a) the extent to which the test items sample the subject-matter field in a balanced fashion and (b) the extent to which the students who take the test have had a fair chance to master the knowledge and skills sampled by the test items. Therefore, two statistical measures of content validity are (a) the percentage of items that measure the test's subject-matter field in a balanced manner and (b) the percentage of items whose content the students have had an adequate opportunity to learn. The higher these percentages are, the more valid the test.

Suitability: The term *suitability* refers to a variety of additional features of a test that influence how accurately the instrument measures what it is intended to assess. Those features include understandable language, clear directions, and comprehensible format.

Understandable language. Unless the test is designed specifically to evaluate students' mastery of vocabulary and grammar, the language used in test items should be readily understood by everyone who takes the test. In other words, the way test items are phrased should not be a barrier to students' revealing their knowledge and skills in such fields as science, math, social studies, literature, and the like.

Clear directions. The oral or written directions about how to take the test should be specific and easy to understand. If the test items are of a type unfamiliar to some students, then the proper way of answering the items should be demonstrated with one or two examples. For instance, a teacher, along with the students, can orally work through the first one or two items in a section of the test to make clear the proper way to proceed.

Comprehensible format. Test-takers' opportunity to show their mastery of the test's content should not be impaired by such format features as (a) crowded test items, (b) too little space for writing answers, (c) small type size, and (d) the awkward placement of diagrams or pictures.

Stages in Creating an Achievement Test

When teachers find no existing test sufficiently reliable, valid, and suitable for their research project, they are obliged to create their own, which in most cases will be an achievement test. Thus, the following discussion focuses solely on achievement tests. Procedures for developing other types (aptitude, intelligence, interest, personality) can be somewhat different.

Our example of stages in creating a test concerns an eighth-grade social-studies teacher's research project in which she wants to discover how effectively students learn about "How Our Community is Governed" during a six-week unit of study taught by a combination of illustrated lectures, discussions, and small-group projects. There are two kinds of learning objectives for the unit: (a) students' knowledge (facts, concepts, generalizations) about how their community is governed and (b) students' investigative skills, in the sense of how to find and interpret information about a topic of interest. The project will assume the form of a *pretest-treatment-posttest* experiment. Two days of pretesting determines what the students know at the outset of the unit about (a) how their community is governed and (b) investigative skills. The treatment involves 26 class periods of lectures/discussions and small-group projects. Two days of posttesting determine what the students know at the close of the six weeks about community governance and investigative skills. The effectiveness of the treatment will be judged by the difference between students' pretest and posttest scores. That is, what the students knew at the beginning of the unit will be subtracted from what they know at the end, in order to show how much they apparently gained during the weeks of instruction.

The teacher plans to develop one pair of tests (consisting of two equivalent forms) to assess students' knowledge (facts, concepts, generalizations) of community governance and another pair (two equivalent forms) to evaluate their investigative skills. Those skills include of ways of (a) selecting the kinds of information needed to answer a research question, (b) identifying sources of such information, (c) collecting and recording the information, and (d) reporting the results.

One form of each pair of tests will be used as a pretest and the other form as a posttest. The pretesting occurs during the first two class periods of the unit, with the governance-knowledge test given the first day and the investigative-skills test the second day. In a similar fashion, the posttesting will take place during the last two class periods of the six-week unit.

The treatment portion of the project will be divided into two equal parts. During the first part, the teacher will conduct daily illustrated-lecture and discussion sessions focusing on the knowledge and skills that students are expected to master. During the second part, students will be divided into groups (four or five students to a group) to gather information about the questions on which the unit focuses and to report their findings in the form of (a) a group paper and (b) a group oral presentation to the class.

The following example illustrates stages through which the teacher progresses in creating the pair of governance-knowledge tests. A similar set of decisions will be appropriate for constructing the equivalent forms of an investigative-methods test.

Stage 1: Specifying the Learning Objectives

Students are to learn facts, concepts, and generalizations within five categories, with the contents of each category reflected in one or more questions:

- *The Division of Responsibilities.* What important responsibilities and powers in governing our community are held by each of the following governmental bodies: federal, state, county, city?
- *Departments of Local Governments.* Into what divisions or departments are our county and city governments divided, what are the responsibilities of each department, how do the departments' personnel get their positions, in what ways may each department influence my life, and how might I influence how each department conducts its business?
- *Finance.* From what sources do our county and city governments get their money, how do they decide how to spend that money, and what can citizens do to influence where the money comes from and how it is spent?

- *Problems.* What important problems do county and city departments face at the present time, what are the main causes of such problems, and what might citizens do to help solve those problems?
- *Occupational Preparation.* After I graduate from high school or college and am looking for an occupation, what kind of training or experience will I need in order to get a position in a county or city department? (Identify six types of positions, describe kinds of skills and knowledge they require, and tell how a person could acquire those skills and knowledge.)

Stage 2: Selecting types of test items

To select the form of test items to use, the teacher considers the characteristics of the following types: true-false, multiple-choice, matching, completion (fill the blanks in sentences), short answer (one to three sentences), essay (extended written explanation), and graphic (the student draws a diagram and labels its parts). Because, within a 50-minute class period, the researcher wishes to sample a wide range of the learners' knowledge about governance, she plans to adopt a single type of item that (a) the students are already familiar with, so they do not need to spend time discovering how to answer new types, and (b) can be answered rather quickly. Thus, she chooses to compose each of the test's two equivalent forms with 40 four-option multiple-choice items.

3. Sampling the learning objectives in a balanced manner

The teacher estimates the comparative importance and complexity of each of the five categories of objectives. On the basis of this estimate, she assigns the number of test items that she believes each category deserves.

The Division of Responsibilities— 6 items
Departments of Local Governments— 12 items
Finance— 4 items
Problems— 13 items
Occupational Preparation— 5 items

4. Creating the test items

From her knowledge of the content of the five categories, the teacher selects a sampling of facts, concepts, and generalizations on which to base multiple-choice items. She will prepare two versions of each item. The students' knowledge that is needed to answer both versions will be the same, but the wording of the items will be different. One version of each pair will be used in the pretest, and the other version in the posttest.

5. Determining the test format

To make the test's layout easy for students to understand, the teacher writes simple directions on how to answer the items, prints the items in a sufficiently large type size, and distributes the items on each page so they are not crowded together.

6. Trying-out the pair of tests

Before using the pair of tests in the experiment, the researcher needs to try-out the initial versions in order to (a) rephrase any items that students would likely misinterpret and (b) ensure that the four alternative answer choices for each multiple-choice item will discriminate accurately between students who truly know the required information and those who simply guess. The teacher does not wish to use her eighth-grade students for this tryout, since doing so would influence the actual experiment. Therefore, she will ask a ninth-grade social-studies teacher to tryout the tests with a ninth-grade class and will solicit those students' opinions about any confusing aspects of the tryout versions.

7. Determining alternate-forms reliability

If, in the tryout that uses ninth-graders, the original versions of the two test forms prove to be generally free of faults, so that no substantial revision of the items or format is required, then the teacher can use the ninth-graders' scores on the alternate versions of the test to calculate how consistently the two forms measure students' command of the learning objectives. In other words, the teacher can calculate how highly one form correlates with the other.

However, if one or both of the versions of the test that the ninth-graders tried out require substantial revision, then the teacher would be wise to have the tryout repeated with other ninth-graders who take the revised pair of tests; and from those scores the teacher would calculate how consistently the two alternate forms measure the same set of knowledge and skills.

8. Administering the final test versions

When the researcher is satisfied that the alternate forms of the test are free of faults and that they provide equivalent measures of how well students have mastered the learning objectives, then one form can serve as the pretest in the experiment with the eighth-graders and the other form as the posttest.

Planning Guide

For a research project that you intend to conduct, or for a project that you can imagine, identify which of these data-collection methods you would plan to use—observations, interviews, questionnaires, content analyses, or tests. Then carry out the following activities that offer you experience with the method or methods that you have selected.

1. *Observations.* In your envisioned project,

    1.1 State the question, or questions, you hope to answer by carrying out observations.

    1.2 Tell who or what you intend to observe, where, and when.

1.3 Describe any equipment you would use to help with your observations, and tell how and why you would use such equipment.

1.4 Tell how you plan to record your observations, when you will do the recording, and why you have chosen such a method.

1.5 Explain your procedure for organizing and summarizing your observations in order to answer the question or questions in item 1.1 above.

2. *Interviews.* For your project,

2.1 State the research question, or questions, that the interviews should help you answer.

2.2 Tell what kind of people you plan to interview, why that kind, and how you will obtain them.

2.3 Describe the explanation you will offer the interviewees when you are soliciting their cooperation and when you open the actual interview.

2.4 Explain the interview strategy—or combination of strategies—that you plan to adopt, and tell why you prefer that approach (loose, tight, converging, response-guided).

2.5 If you intend to use equipment in conducting interviews, describe that equipment and tell why you will use it (audio-recorder, video-recorder, or the like).

2.6 Describe your method—or methods—of recording the content of the interview, and explain why you have chosen such a method.

2.7 Explain the procedure you will use to organize the results of the interviews in order to answer the question or questions in item 2.1 above.

3. *Questionnaires.* In your plan to collect data by means of a questionnaire,

3.1 State the research question, or questions, that the questionnaire should help you answer.

3.2 Tell to whom the questionnaire will be sent, explain why such people are appropriate participants for your project, and tell how you will locate such participants.

3.3 Explain what considerations you will have in mind when you plan the questionnaire format and write the items (considerations about the nature of the participants and the setting in which they will be expected to complete the questionnaire).

3.4 Write the questionnaire.

3.5 Describe how, when, and where the questionnaire will be administered to the participants.

3.6 Tell what means you will use to encourage participants to complete the questionnaire and return it to you.

3.7 Describe the procedure you intend to follow in tabulating the returned questionnaires and organizing the results in order to answer the question or questions in item 3.1 above.

4. *Content analyses.* For your research plan that includes gathering information by content analysis,

4.1 State the research question, or questions, that the results of the analysis should help you answer.

4.2 Describe the kinds of communications that you hope to analyze.

4.3 Identify the sources from which you hope to obtain the communications (World Wide Web, library books, professional journals, newspapers, collections of letters, or the like).

4.4 List key words or phrases that can guide your search of the Web, of library computer catalogues, of book indexes, of newspaper archives, and the like.

4.5 For each type of information source that you intend to use, describe the method—or methods—you will use to record information gathered during your analysis.

4.6 Tell how you plan to summarize the results of your analysis in order to answer the question or questions in item 4.1 above.

5. *Tests.* To identify the manner in which one or more tests will serve in your project,

5.1 State the research question, or questions, that the test results should help you answer.

5.2 Identify the kinds of people who will be taking the test, and describe their characteristics that should influence the form of the test and its mode of administration so as to yield an accurate measure of the knowledge, skills, or personality features that the test is supposed to assess.

5.3 In view of your answers in 5.1 and 5.2, describe the types of items that will comprise the test (multiple-choice, essay, or the like), the number of items, and the way the test will be administered.

5.4 Create the test, and explain how its items sample its field of focus in a balanced fashion.

5.5 Describe the way you will compile and report the results of testing so as to answer the question or questions from item 5.1.

7

Organizing Information

The expression *raw data* refers to the form of information that has been collected for the purpose of answering a project's research questions. Here are some examples of raw data.

- Questionnaires filled out by 127 parents, concerning their opinions of the type and frequency of homework assigned to pupils, grades 4 through 6
- Language-arts achievement tests (reading speed and comprehension, spelling, grammar, punctuation) completed by 1,300 middle-school students
- Audiotapes of 43 interviews with high-school students who described their reactions to a shooting incident in their school
- Handwritten notes taken by a teacher during her observations of the social behavior of third-graders during the children's rehearsals for a school play
- Articles copied from the Internet and entered into a computer file during a teacher's search of the World Wide Web for moral-education learning activities appropriate for secondary-school students
- A diary and a collection of letters written over a period of three decades by a highly regarded high-school choral director whose biography is being prepared as a master's-degree thesis project
- Annual enrollment figures in foreign-language classes in a city school system during the period 1950-2000
- Videotapes of 23 students giving first-week and sixteenth-week speeches in front of their class

The purpose of this chapter is to describe ways that raw data can be organized and presented so that readers of a research report gain a clear, convincing understanding of how the data answer the research study's focal questions. The first portion of the chapter treats classification systems. The second portion concerns statistical forms of presenting information, and the third concerns graphic methods.

Classification Systems

Every research effort employs a system for placing people, objects, and episodes in categories in order to compare them or to arrange them in an understandable sequence. Such systems are often called *typologies, taxonomies,* or *classificatory schemes.* The following discussion of typologies addresses matters of (a) kinds of classification schemes, (b) finding a suitable scheme, and (c) classification systems' structures.

Kinds of Classification Systems

Among the most frequent ways of classifying things are schemes based on distinctions of quality, of quantity, of sequence, or of some combination of quality, quantity, and sequence.

Qualitative schemes: In a qualitative system, the differences between classes are distinctions of *kind* rather than amount. For instance, a way of categorizing equine-like quadrupeds uses the animals' observable features for defining classes that distinguish among palominos, Clydesdales, quarter horses, pintos, and zebras. Animals that display the same kinds of features are assigned to the same class.

The following qualitative schemes are often used in educational research.

Gender—male and female
Ethnic status—Black, White, Native American, Asian, Hispanic
Religion—Protestant, Roman Catholic, Islamic, Jewish, Hindu, Atheist
Language spoken at home—English, Spanish, Chinese, Japanese, Samoan
Parent's occupation—professional, managerial, skilled craft, service, home-
    maker
Academic major—science, social science, English, music, art, industrial arts
Handwriting—illegible, difficult to read, legible, consistent, elegant
Moral-education learning activities—storybooks, news analyses, moral dilem-
    mas, personal anecdotes, sociodramas, social-action projects
Social behaviors—aggression, ostracism, friendly overtures, competition, co-
    operation, self isolation

Quantitative schemes: Quantitative systems distinguish between classes in terms of amounts, frequencies, or magnitudes, such as,

Number of correct test items—25-30, 20-24, 15-19, 10-14, 5-9, 0-4
Percent of correct test items—95-100%, 90-94%, 85-89%, 80-84%, 75-79%, 70-
    75%, etc.
Percents translated into letter grades—90-100%=**A**, 80-89%=**B**, 70-79%=**C**, 60-
    69%=**D**, 0-59%=**F**
Unexcused absences—None, 1-4, 5-8, 9-12, 13-or-more

Sequential schemes: A sequential system involves classes defined by the order in which events occur.

Ordered by years—1996, 1997, 1998, 1999, 2000, 2001, 2002, 2003
Ordered by months— September, October, November, December
Ordered by events—pretest, one-month-training session, immediate posttest, three-month posttest, six-month posttest
Steps in a process—Teacher fills out textbook order, textbook order is sent to the principal, the principal locates textbook sources, criteria are applied in choosing among sources, the principal fills out a requisition form, the order is sent to the selected source, books are delivered to the school, books are delivered to the teacher, books are distributed to students

Combination schemes: Some systems combine features of quality and/or quantity and/or sequence.

Quality, quantity—The frequency of each child's displaying the following reactions to criticism or to correction by the teacher: (a) denies any fault, (b) offers excuses, (c) blames others, (d) sulks, (e) apologizes, (f) promises to do better
Quality, quantity, sequence—The number of errors in each student's essay in terms of (a) spelling, (b) punctuation, (c) capitalization, (d) noun-verb agreement, and (e) logical order of ideas

Finding a Suitable Classification Scheme

The nature of the classification method needed for a research study is usually implied in the questions the study is intended to answer, as illustrated in Table 7-1, where the questions are listed in the left column and their appropriate classification schemes in the right column. Each scheme is defined in terms of the variables or categories into which the researcher's typology is divided. Identifying those categories early in the process of planning the project aids the researcher in choosing an efficient form in which to gather and record data. For instance, consider the first example in which the question to be answered is: Do elementary-school pupils from one-parent homes get into more trouble in school than ones from two-parent homes? To answer this question, the researcher needs two sorts of information: (a) which pupils are from one-parent homes and which are from two-parent homes and (b) how much "trouble" the different pupils "get into" in school. In addition, let's assume that the researcher also wonders about a possible connection between "trouble-making" and a pupil's (c) grade level and (d) gender. Thus, the information needed about each pupil becomes four-fold.

Table 7-1

Research Questions and Classification Categories

Research Question	*Appropriate Classification Scheme*
Do elementary-school pupils from one-parent homes get into more trouble in school than ones from two-parent homes?	(1) Different types of "trouble," by (2) one-parent and two-parent homes, by (3) grade level, and by (4) gender.
At successive stages of her life, who influenced the development of Jean Wellington as an author of children's books?	(1) Different individuals, by (2) kind and amount of influence, by (3) stages of the lifespan.
How did enrollments in the city's high-school foreign-language classes change over the 50-year era 1950-2000?	(1) Languages, by (2) levels of language competence (introductory versus advanced), by (3) five-year periods
How much progress in public speaking did students achieve over a 16-week period, as judged by their videotaped speeches?	(1) First-week vs. sixteenth week, by (2) quality of speech (organization of ideas, vocabulary, volume, enunciation, distractive mannerisms, posture)
What was the success of 1,300 middle-school students on a battery of language-arts tests?	(1) Grade (seventh, eighth, ninth), by (2) school (Central, Lincoln, Grant), by (3) gender, by (4) type of skill (reading speed and comprehension, spelling, grammar, punctuation)
What are the reactions of students to the shooting incident in their high school?	(1) Source of a student's information about the shooting (was shot, witnessed shooting, hearsay), (2) type of reaction, (3) connection with shooter, (4) connection with victims, (5) action taken at the time of the shooting, (6) gender

Classification Systems' Structures

Typologies can be cast in various forms. Three of the most common forms can be labeled *intuitive, outline,* and *tabular.*

An intuitive typology consists of categories that an author has in mind, probably at a subconscious level rather than being intentionally chosen. In other words, by virtue of intuition, the researcher "has a sense of" what to write about—a kind of unplanned, instinctive insight into how best to explain the events that are being studied. Hence, the classes in a intuitive typology are not specified nor is the relationship among the classes described. Research projects that most often depend on intuitive typologies are histories, biographies, case studies, ethnographies, and experience narratives.

Typologies in outline form, in contrast to intuitive classification schemes, explicitly display the system's classes and their interrelationships as major categories that subsume various levels of minor categories. Typologies in tabular form do the same, but portray the classes as items in a table rather than in an outline. Both outline and tabular typologies are typically found in research projects involving surveys, correlational studies, and experiments. However, authors of histories, biographies, case studies, and ethnographies may also openly specify the classes that comprise their projects' organizational structure.

One way of constructing outline and tabular typologies is illustrated in the following four-step process as applied to three sample research projects—(a) the biography of an art teacher (outline), (b) a study of students' friendships in a junior high school (outline), and (c) an experiment in teaching high school American history (tabular).

Step 1: Specify the questions that the research is designed to answer.

Biography: Rita Viccini, Artist and Educator
Question: What factors in Rita Viccini's life significantly influenced her career choice and her remarkable success as both an artist and an art teacher?

Friendship-study: Friendship Patterns in a Multicultural Junior High
Question: What characteristics do friends share in common? Which schoolmates would students like to have as friends and why?

History-teaching: Understanding History: Videotapes Versus Textbooks
Question: How effectively do students in a high-school American history class learn about significant historical events (what occurred) and the events' interpretation (causes and consequences) by means of a videotape/discussion method versus a textbook/discussion method?

Step 2: Describe the kinds of information to be collected to answer the questions.

(a) *Biography.* (A) Interviews with Rita Viccini, with people who have known her, and with people acquainted with her paintings and with the work of her students
(B) Newspaper and magazine articles about Ms. Viccinni.
(C) Photographs of Ms. Viccini's paintings and her students' art products

(b) *Friendship.* (A) A Friendship-Choices survey form that students fill out to show which schoolmates they regard as their friends and which ones they would like to have as friends
(B) Observations of social interactions among students in terms of the interactions' frequency, length, quality, and kinds of occasions
(C) Information about students' gender, ethnic status, socioeconomic level, religious affiliation, and personality traits

(c) *History.* (A) Pretest and posttest scores from the two major sections of a history test—one section assessing knowledge of events, the other assessing knowledge of interpretations
(B) The treatment (videotape/discussion or textbook/discussion) in which different students participated

Step 3: Determine the form of the classification categories.

(a) *Biography.* The author's intention is to trace the apparent influential people and events in Ms. Viccini's life from her childhood through her active years as an artist/teacher and into her years of retirement. Thus, information can be efficiently classified by (A) stages of her life and (B) types of influence within each stage.

(b) *Friendship.* The purpose of the research is to reveal (A) students' actual friendships, and the attributes students value in those friends, (B) friendships students would like to have, (C) characteristics students share with actual friends, and (D) characteristics students admire in people they would like to have as friends. Because the junior high school that the students attend is multicultural, the researcher is particularly interested in the effect on friendship patterns of such characteristics as (E) gender, (F) ethnic status, (G) socioeconomic level, (H) religious affiliation, and (I) individuals' personality traits. Therefore, information will classified by each of the above variables: A-through-I.

The results of observations of students' social interactions will be classified by interactions' (J) frequency, (K) length, (L) quality, and (M) kinds of occasions.

(c) *History.* The teacher not only wishes to learn the level of students' success under the two treatments (videotape/discussion versus textbook/discussion), but also what difference, if any, exists between girls and boys in their test performance under the two treatment conditions. Therefore, classification categories will include (A) pretest scores, (B) posttest scores, and (C) change scores (posttest minus pretest) by (D) types of treatment and (E) gender.

Step 4: Identify the source of the classification system's categories. The classes or categories within a typology can be either preconceived or data-generated. Preconceived categories are ones the researcher determines before collecting information and classifying it. Data-generated categories (grounded categories) are created only after the information has been collected and inspected. These two sources may be combined whenever the researcher estimates, prior to collecting data, what the final classes will be, but then alters the classes after analyzing the data; that is, after gathering data, the researcher readjusts the classes so as to answer the research questions more precisely.

(a) *Biography.* Preconceived categories: Before collecting information, the researcher divides Ms. Vinccini's life into five life stages.

> Childhood (birth through age 11)
> Adolescence (age 12 through 20)
> Early adulthood (21 through 35)
> Middle adulthood (36 through 64)
> Retirement (65+)

Such a division is based on the investigator's estimate about when in the artist's lifespan different sources of influence most significantly affected her career. Then, under each of the life stages, there will be two primary categories—influential people and influential incidents—with the subcategories under each of these generated out of the data.

Data-generated categories: During the process of collecting information about Ms. Viccini's life, the researcher begins to identify specific people and incidents that apparently had exerted a significant effect on the artist's career. Because simply listing the people and incidents would become unduly awkward to write about, the researcher plans to combine the specific ones into subcategories. For example, the outline under the adolescent life-stage might look something like this:

2. Adolescence
  2.1 Significant people
    2.1.1 Family members
    2.1.2 Teachers
    2.1.3 Friends, acquaintances
    2.1.4 People she knew about and admired but did not know personally

  2.2 Significant incidents
    2.2.1 Art classes
    2.2.2 Art exhibits and shows she attended
    2.2.3 Art competitions in which she participated
    2.2.4 Her appointment to positions as a teacher or artist
    2.2.5 Her encounters with other artists and her own students

Beneath each of the other four life stages, significant people and incidents would also be identified, with the subclasses below those two categories likely varying somewhat from those under *Adolescence* because of the nature of the woman's experiences during different periods of her life.

(b) *Friendship.* Preconceived categories: The classes the researcher initially establishes for each student are as follows:

(A) Friends: Schoolmates that a student lists as friends.

(B) Wished-for friends: Schoolmates a student would like as friends.

(C) Gender of the student and gender of actual and wished-for friends

(D) Ethnic status of the student and of actual and wished-for friends

(E) Socioeconomic level of the student and of actual and wished-for friends

(F) Religious affiliation of the student and of actual and wished-for friends

Data-generated categories: After the data have been gathered, the set of classes under each of the following types of data will be established from an analysis of the information that has been gathered about each type. Thus, for each student there will be categories of:

(G) Personality traits of friends (from the Friendship Choices survey and the researcher's observations)

(H) Personality traits of wished-for friends (from the survey results and observations)

(I) Social interaction (from observations)

(I-1) With whom

(I-2) Nature of occasion

(I-3) Frequency of interaction

(I-4) Length of interaction

(I-5) Quality of interaction

(c) *History.* To answer the research question, data in the history-teaching project can be conveniently cast as a table that identifies where numbers will be entered for answering the question about students' success in relation to (a) the teaching method they experienced and (b) their gender (Table 7-2).

Conclusion

Finally, a question can be asked about why a researcher should bother to create an intentional, formally described classification system when an intuitive approach might seem good enough. The answer is that a formally described scheme (a) clearly identifies the kinds of information the researcher should collect and (b) helps readers of the research understand the pattern of categories into which the data have been organized. An intuitive, unmindful, approach lacks these advantages.

Table 7-2

Table of Classification Categories for the History-Teaching Project

Students' Knowledge of Historical Events

	Video/Discussion Method			*Textbook/Discussion Method*		
	Girls	*Boys*	*Total*	*Girls*	*Boys*	*Total*
Pretest scores						
Posttest scores						
Change scores (Post minus Pre)						

Students' Knowledge of Historical Interpretations

	Video/Discussion Method			*Textbook/Discussion Method*		
	Girls	*Boys*	*Total*	*Girls*	*Boys*	*Total*
Pretest scores						
Posttest scores						
Change scores (Post minus Pre)						

Descriptive Statistics

The term *descriptive statistics* refers to numerical methods for summarizing information about individuals or groups. In contrast, the expression *inferential statistics* refers to numerical ways of estimating how likely the description of an individual or group that was studied can be validly applied to other individuals or groups that were not studied. The distinction between these two terms can be illustrated with an example of the kinds of research questions to be answered.

Descriptive statistics: How well did ninth-graders in School A succeed in physical-fitness tests?

Inferential statistics: How probable is it that the pattern of scores of all ninth-graders in our state would be the same (if all students were tested) as the pattern of the scores earned by School-A students?

The following section is devoted solely to descriptive statistics. The matter of inferential statistics is addressed in Chapter 8 which focuses on ways of interpreting research results.

Two general advantages of descriptive statistics over verbal descriptions are those of economy and precision.

Economy refers to the ability of statistics to convey a host of information in a concise fashion. For instance, if we wish to know the general success of 150 seventh-graders on a 100-point reading-comprehension test, our wish is more economically fulfilled if we learn that the group's average was 73.5 than if we simply have a list of the 150 students' individual scores to inspect. We also find it helpful to discover that 68% of our 150 students scored above the average (64 points) of a nationwide sample of 87,000 seventh graders.

In addition, statistics offer greater *precision* than do verbal accounts. Reporting that the 150 students' test scores extended from the lowest of 29 to the highest of 93 (a range of 64 points) is more precise than saying that "there was a lot of variability among the students" or "the scores really spread out." .

However, an important shortcoming of statistical summaries is that they fail to portray the intricate pattern of an individual person's or group's life, a pattern that can be revealed only in a verbal account, such as in (a) a case study of the behvior expected of girls in an Chinese-immigrant family or (b) an ethnographic analysis of teacher-student interactions in a high-school physical-education class.

Among many available kinds of statistics, the ones typically most useful for the research that teachers conduct are (a) frequencies, (b) percentages and percentiles, (c) indicators of central tendency, (d) indicators of variability, and (e) indicators of correlation. The following brief sketch of these types focuses on their uses, advantages, limitations, and sources of information about how to calculate them. In the sketch, the way each type can be used in a particular research project is illustrated with a study of sixth-graders' performance on a geography test in three elementary schools—Adams, Beach, and Central. Each school had three sixth-grade classes. The test consisted of 60 questions, with each question worth one point. The number of students taking the test in Adams School was 73, in Beach 72, and in Central 71.

Raw Data

The following display of scores for the 73 Adams students illustrates the difficulty of understanding how the sixth-graders succeeded on the test when the scores are offered as raw data—as an unorganized list.

Adams School scores: 32, 26, 38, 33, 34, 30, 21, 29, 34, 34, 32, 40, 44, 21, 32, 31, 33, 27, 35, 38, 32, 32, 33, 41, 25, 32, 33, 34, 28, 33, 26, 32, 32, 30, 33, 32, 33, 33, 40, 35, 30, 30, 31, 32, 32, 29, 30, 35, 32, 33, 32, 41, 30, 29, 28, 34, 34, 27, 33, 37, 38, 30, 31, 30, 35, 32, 33, 32, 31, 34, 33, 32, 37.

Figure 7-1

Organizing Test Scores by Means of a Tally Sheet

Test Scores	Adams School	Beach School	Central School
45		/	/
44	/	//	//
43		/	/
42		///	///
41	//	//	/
40	//	///// ///	/////
39		///// ///// /	//
38	///	///// ///// /////	//
37	//	///// ///	/
36		///	/////
35	////	///// //	///// //
34	///// //	///	///// ///
33	///// ///// /		////
32	///// ///// ///// /	/	/
31	/////		///
30	///// ///	//	/
29	///		//
28	//	/	///
27	//		/////
26	//		/////
25	/	/	//
24			/
23			//
22			//
21	/	/	//
20	/		

Frequencies

One simple way to organize a conglomeration of measures is to report them as frequencies showing how often each score, person, object, or event occurred. Figure 7-1 shows how this can be done with a tally sheet that displays the results of geography testing in the three schools.

The tally sheet reveals, at a glance, that School-B students generally succeeded better than students in Schools A and C. And it's easy to recognize that the bulk of the scores in School C were spread across a greater range than in A and B. Frequencies have the advantage of being easy to calculate and easy for readers to understand. However, frequencies can be misleading when two or more groups that are being compared are different in the total number of individuals they contain. For example, we may learn that in School X, there are 17 kindergarten children whose families are on welfare rolls, whereas in School Y there are 16 such children. Thus, we might assume that the incidence of poverty was nearly the same in the two schools—until we discover that the total number of kindergarteners in School X is 27 and in School Y is 48.

Percentages and Percentiles

Percentages furnish a familiar way to report the proportion of people or events that displayed some characteristic, such as:

- The proportion of students earning A's at Lincoln High School in 2003 compared to the proportions in 1983 and 1993
- The proportion of times a student was absent during the school year
- The frequency with which high-school math students turned in homework on time
- The degree of increase in teachers' salaries between 1994 and 2004.

An important advantage of percentages is that they can convert diverse forms of information (such as frequencies based on different totals of events) into a single form—into a common coin—that virtually everybody can understand. Thus, reporting that the families of 17 kindergarten children are on welfare tells less about the incidence of poverty among pupils' families than does reporting that 63% of children's families are welfare recipients. And learning that 16 children's families are on the welfare rolls tells less about the comparative incidence of poverty among School X and School Y kindergarteners than does the information that 33% of children in School Y are from families on welfare.

In the case of the geography testing of Adams, Beach, and Central pupils, we could report that 72% of the sixth-graders in Adams correctly answered more than half of the test questions (31 or more of the 60 test items), whereas 93% correctly answered more than half in Beach and 65% in Central.

When interpreting statistical reports, people sometimes confuse the meanings of *percentages* and *percentiles*. They fail to recognize that a percentage identifies the proportion of a given characteristic within group of things, whereas a percentile is the point below which a particular proportion of the characteristic falls. Thus, in Beach School, a sixth-grader named Alex accurately answered 36 of the test's 60 items; so he was correct on 60% of the questions. Now we wish to learn where, out of the 72 Beach sixth-graders, Alex ranked in terms of success on the test when compared with his schoolmates. To discover that, we list the students in the order of their test scores from the lowest to the highest (as in Figure 7-1) and then find Alex's rank. We note that Alex is the 18th student up the list or the 53rd from the top. We calculate his percentile by dividing 18 by 72 to learn that he is at the 25th percentile. In short, he is at the point below which 25% of his classmates scored. If Alex had been in Central School and had earned a score of 36, he would have ranked as the 50th student from the bottom of the distribution and at the 70th percentile among the Central School sixth-graders. Therefore, the percentage of test items Alex answered correctly would have been the same, no matter which school he attended. But his percentile rank could differ from one school to another, as governed by how well he succeeded on the test in relation to the other students with whom he was compared.

Indicators of Central Tendency

Researchers frequently wish to answer—in the form of a single number—such questions as "How did the class do in general on the safety-practices test?" or "On the average, how long did it take for teachers to receive a reply from the district office?" or "Across the entire semester, how well did Carmelita succeed with her homework assignments?"

The two most popular statistics for reporting such central tendencies are the *arithmetic mean* and the *median*. The mean is computed by adding up the individual instances (the class members' test scores, how many days passed before teachers got replies from the office, Carmelita's scores on the semester's homework assignments) and dividing that sum by the total number of instances (the number of students who took the test, the number of communications sent to the office, the number of homework assignments). The median, in contrast, is the mid-point in a list of ranks that extend from the smallest to the largest (test scores, number of days for a response from the office, scores on homework assignments). In other words, the median is the same as the 50th percentile—the halfway point in a distribution of things that are ranked from the lowest to the highest.

Consider, now, the question: "In general, how did the students in Adams, Beach, and Central schools compare in their performance on the geography test?" By inspecting Figure 7-1, we can easily see that the Beach students were considerably better than either the Adams or Central students. But it is not clear which school, Adams or Central, was next best until we compute the mean or median to arrive at the following figures:

School	Mean	Median
Adams	32.3	32
Beach	37.5	38
Central	32.8	34

We now have a more precise understanding of how the three groups compared "in general" or "on the average." We recognize that Beach was about five points higher than the other two schools and that Central was slightly ahead of Adams.

Finally, which of these two measures—mean or median—is the better one to report? The answer depends on several factors. First is the matter of ease. The median usually is the simpler one to compute, for it merely involves finding the middle score in a distribution of scores. However, if additional, more advanced statistics (standard deviation, standard error, and others) will later be computed, the mean is the one to adopt.

Indicators of Variability

Reporting only the central tendency—mean or medium—of a group of measures is seldom sufficient for describing the nature of a group. It is also desirable to indicate the extent of variability within the group, that is, how widely the measures spread out from the center.

Perhaps the most obvious measure of dispersion is the *range*, which is defined as the distance between the lowest and highest amount in a distribution. In Figure 7-1, when we subtract the lowest score from the highest in the three schools' distributions, we discover that the range is the same in each school—44 points. However, reporting that the three schools were exactly the same in the way the students' scores in general spread out from the center would be misleading, indeed. The problem with the range is that it is determined by only two scores, the highest and the lowest, whereas what we want to convey is an impression of how the "scores in general" or the "bulk of the scores" were dispersed. There are two popular ways to do this, with each of the ways allied to our two central-tendency statistics, the mean and the median.

The *standard deviation* is the measure of variability paired with, and dependent on, the mean. It is calculated by finding the average of how far squared scores deviate from the mean. (Calculation methods are found in nearly all introductory statistics textbooks.) When two or more groups are being compared, the group with the largest standard deviation is the one whose scores, in general, are spread out farthest from the mean. Calculating standard deviations for the three schools in Figure 7-1 results in the following figures:

School	Standard Deviation
Adams	4.07
Beach	3.97
Central	6.27

Whereas inspecting the tally sheet in Figure 7-1 shows clearly that the scores in Central School varied the most, it is difficult to determine whether the spread of scores in Adams was greater or smaller than in Beach. But the standard deviations for the two schools furnish us a precise answer to this quandary: the Adam's scores spread out slightly more than the Beach scores.

Consider now some measures of dispersion that are allied to the median, measures referred to as *differences between percentiles.* You may recall the misunderstanding that can result from using the range to represent the variability of a distribution; that is, the range is determined entirely by one extreme high score and one extreme low score. So, to avoid the influence of unusually high or low scores on the impression we give of the dispersion of the bulk of the measures in a distribution, we can cut off a portion of the lower and of the upper extremes of the distribution and report how much the remaining central cluster of scores spread out. Imagine that we want to cut off the bottom 10% and top 10% of scores for each of the three schools in Figure 7-1 and to report the distance covered by the resulting inner 80% of the distributions. We do this for Adams School by counting 10% of the students (7 students) up from the bottom of the Adams distribution to arrive at score 26 and by counting 10% (7 students) down from the top to score 38. Then 16 is subtracted from 38 to yield a distance between percentiles of 22. We do the same for the Beach and Central distributions. Or, if we wish to remove even more of the extreme scores—say, 15% at the bottom and top—we could report the distance between the 15th percentile (15%ile) and the 85%ile and report the spread of the inner 70% of the scores. Doing so produces the following figures.

School	Distance between Percentiles	
	90%ile minus 10%ile =	85%ile minus 15%ile =
Adams	38 – 27 = 11	35 – 29 = 6
Beach	42 – 34 = 8	41 – 35 = 6
Central	41 – 24 = 17	40 – 26 = 14

The variability comparison among the three schools, as told by the distance-between-percentiles approach, is essentially the same as that told by the standard deviation—the bunching together of the bulk of the scores was greater in Adams and Beach than in Central, where the scores stretched over a greater distance.

Another statistic that some people use is the *interquartile range*. As its title implies, it reports the distance between the 25%ile and 75%ile, thereby representing the spreading out of the inner 50% of scores. When the interquartile range is divided by two, it yields what is referred to as the *semi-interquartile range*.

School	Interquartile Range 75%ile minus 25%ile =
Adams	34 – 30 = 4
Beach	40 – 36 = 6
Central	37 – 27 = 10

In summary, a percentile approach can be adopted to represent the dispersion—or bunching together—of the measures used in a research project. Which percentiles will be used for calculating the distance between percentiles depends on the researcher's decision about what proportion of the extreme scores—high and low—should be eliminated in order to furnish a convincing view of the variability of a group of scores or other measures.

Indicators of Correlation

In Chapter 5 the meaning of statistical correlation was discussed in some detail, and readers were directed to textbooks that explain a variety of methods for calculating the degree of relationship among variables. Thus, there is no need to repeat such information here. The only point about correlation that I wish to make at this juncture is that numerical descriptions of relationships—as shown in a Pearson or a Spearman correlation coefficient—provide a more precise understanding of the degree of relationship between variables than do such verbal descriptions as "Physical fitness and dietary habits are closely connected" or "Academic success and skill in driving a car are entirely separate entities."

Further Sources of Statistical Procedures

Typical introductory statistics textbooks not only describe the methods of calculating measures of central tendency, variability, and correlation, but they describe a variety of additional statistical procedures as well, including the advantages, limitations, and suitable applications of those procedures. The following are examples of such resources:

Glass, G. V., & Hopkins, K. D. (1996). *Statistical Methods in Education and Psychology* (3rd ed.). Boston: Allyn & Bacon.

Gravetter, F. J. (1988). *Statistics for the Behavioral Sciences.* St. Paul, MN: West.

Hays, W. L. (1994). *Statistics* (5th ed.). Fort Worth, TX: Harcourt Brace.

Jaccard, J., & Becker, M. A. (1990). *Statistics for the Behavioral Sciences* (2nd ed.). Belmont, CA: Wadsworth.

Popham, W. J., & Sirotnkik, K. A. (1992). *Understanding Statistics in Education.* Itasca, IL: Peacock.

Siegel, S., & Castellan, N. J., Jr. (1988). *Nonparametric Statistics for the Behavioral Sciences* (2nd ed.). New York: McGraw-Hill.

Sprinthall, R. C. (1997). *Basic Statistical Analysis* (5th ed.). Boston, MA: Allyn & Bacon.

Graphic Displays

Tables, charts, and graphs—as devices for classifying information—have the advantage of presenting a host of data and their interrelationships simultaneously rather than requiring readers to accumulate such information in the step-by-step pattern of a verbal description. Graphic displays are also more efficient for conveying complex relationships among data than are single-number statistics, such as percentages, means, standard deviations, and correlation coefficients.

The following section illustrates the advantages of tabular and graphic presentations with examples from types of research reports that teachers may conduct. Eight kinds of displays are included—tables, pie graphs, bar charts, time lines, trend graphs, organization charts, flow charts, and maps.

Tables

Tables consist of items arranged in rows and columns. The data can be presented as a simple list of one kind of item—such as a list of schools, of pupils, of teachers, or of textbook titles. Or the table can assume the form of a matrix with more than one variable along each axis. Such a matrix is shown in Table 7-3, where both grade and gender are cast as columns while school district and school are cast as rows. Using the rows to represent the more numerous variables (three districts and 10 schools) makes more efficient use of the page arrangement in a research report than does assigning the more numerous variables to the columns, and thereby unduly crowding the variables across the width of the page.

A narrative accompanying Table 7-3 can direct readers' attention to significant features of the data. For example, girls tended to score slightly higher than boys at the third-grade level in districts 3 and 8.

However, at the sixth-grade level in all three districts, boys scored slightly higher than girls. In addition, the lowest (Bayside) and the highest (Carton and Elm Grove) scores occurred in the same district (District 8) at both the third-grade and sixth-grade levels.

Table 7-3

Average* Math Test Scores in Two School Districts

	Grade 3			Grade 6		
	Boys	Girls	All	Boys	Girls	All
District 3						
J. Q. Adams School	62	72	67	81	79	80
M. L. King School	58	64	61	84	82	83
J. F. Kennedy School	67	69	68	82	84	83
District 3 Average	62.3	68.3	65.3	82.3	81.7	82
District 7						
Oakdale School	51	47	49	64	60	62
East Lane School	48	41	45	58	64	61
Central School	57	61	59	73	70	72
El Monte School	61	58	60	76	74	75
District 7 Average	54.3	51.8	53.3	67.8	67.0	67.5
District 8						
Carlton School	73	73	73	84	82	83
Elm Grove School	70	76	73	86	87	87
Bayside School	56	60	58	70	66	68
District 8 Average	66.3	69.7	68.0	80.0	78.3	79.3
Districts Combined	61.0	63.3	62.2	76.7	75.7	76.3

Note: Potential scores ranged from 0 to 100. More advanced mathematical operations were included on the sixth-grade test than on the third-grade test.

* The table reports the arithmetic means for the listed groups.

Pie Graphs

Pie graphs are convenient devices for conveying at a glance the proportionate contribution of each element to a phenomenon of interest. In Figure 7-2, that phenomenon is the home language of students who attend an urban public school in Southwestern United States. The term *home language,* as intended in this project, is the language most often spoken among the student's family members.

Figure 7-2

The Dominant Language Spoken in Students' Homes

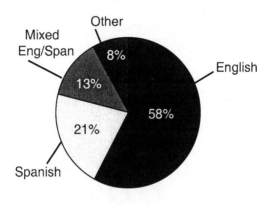

Bar Charts

Bar charts (*histograms*) are useful for showing different frequencies of things that can vary in quality, time, or type. In Figure 7-3, the "thing" is the quality of 72 eighth-graders' performance on a social-studies test that a researcher created as one of the tests to use for investigating differences among students in their patterns of success across five subject-matter areas—reading, writing, math, science, and social studies.

When the researcher devised the 59-item test, she intended to include items of different levels of difficulty (easy, moderate, hard) so as to distinguish among students whose grasp of social-studies facts, concepts, and skills was rather weak, moderate, and strong. She displayed her expectation of the test results as the upper histogram in Figure 7-3. However, after the tests had been administered and scored, the results formed the pattern shown in the lower bar chart of Figure 7-3.

Not only did the least successful student score lower than the researcher had expected, but 10 students had perfect or near-perfect scores. Thus, the investigator could not imagine that all 10 were precisely alike in their command of social studies. In other words, she decided that her test had failed to distinguish different levels of competence among the 10 most successful students. She had not included enough difficult items on the test (in other words, there was not enough "top" on the test) to sufficiently challenge the most competent eighth graders. Therefore, she planned to create an entirely new test that would include some more demanding items and to administer it again.

Casting the expected and actual results as bar graphs made it easy for the teacher and her colleagues to see at a glance the apparent shortcomings of the test.

Figure 7-3

Expected and Actual Results of Social-Studies Testing

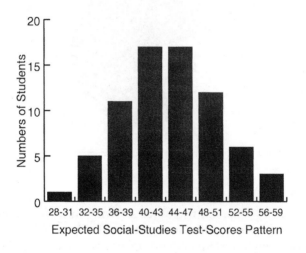

Expected Social-Studies Test-Scores Pattern

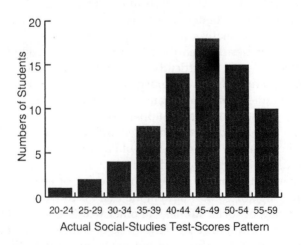

Actual Social-Studies Test-Scores Pattern

Time Lines

A time line portrays chronological relationships among events. Compared with verbal descriptions, time lines are more effective for delineating the length of periods between events and for displaying all events simultaneously. The example in Figure 7-4 is from a biographical sketch prepared when a notably successful teacher and basketball coach was retiring from coaching. The items on the line are events that the author of the biography selected as particularly significant for representing the first six decades of the subject's life.

Figure 7-4

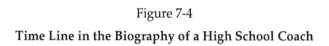

Time Line in the Biography of a High School Coach

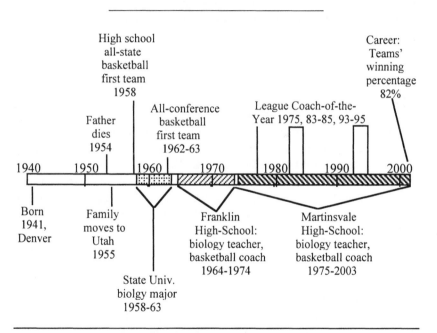

Time lines are especially useful in historical research, as in tracing the history of a particular school, of a teacher's union, of the use of technology in a school district, of a department in a school (home economics, foreign languages, business practices), of special-education, of counseling services, and the like.

Trend Graphs

The purpose of a trend graph is to depict the pattern in which some phenomenon developed with the passing of time. Figure 7-5 traces changes in the actual numbers of students enrolled in the public schools of a West Coast seaside town from 1900 until 2000. The graph then continues with an estimate of enrollments over the next three decades—2000-2030. The purpose of the research was to provide the school district's administrators with information that would aid them in projecting their needs in the coming years.

The graph is accompanied by a narrative explaining that the modest growth during the first half of the 20th century changed dramatically after 1950 as the result of several events. One such event was World War II, which brought army recruits from all parts of the United States to a large training camp located near the town. Following the war, substantial numbers of the former trainees recalled the attractive climate and setting of the West Coast seaside region and moved to the town. The rapid influx of young families over the next quarter century increased the school-age population at a rapid pace. However, by the mid-1980s, a chronic water shortage in the area resulted in restrictions on the number of new homes that could be built. Consequently, the price of existing homes began to rise rapidly as the competition for housing increased. With housing prices rising, fewer young adults could afford to buy a home in the town, so the child-rearing population began to drop significantly. When school planners analyzed the trend factors operating throughout the 1990s, they estimated that those factors (fewer young families, rapidly increasing housing costs) would continue into the future, resulting in the estimated trend for the 2000-2030 period.

Organization Charts

Diagrams depicting the components of an organization are useful in delineating how the various parts of a social structure are related to each other. The example in Figure 7-6 is from a study of a student-operated biweekly newspaper in a large suburban high school. The four-fold purpose of the study was to (a) describe the positions on the newspaper staff and the power/communication connections among the positions, (b) identify problems met in publishing and distributing the paper, (3) estimate the causes of those problems, and (d) suggest ways that such problems might be avoided or satisfactorily resolved.

As in most organization charts, the positions that are assigned the most power of decision are located higher in the chart than positions assigned less power. Likewise, the lines connecting positions indicate the officially recognized channels of communication and control.

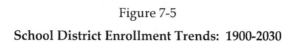

Figure 7-5

School District Enrollment Trends: 1900-2030

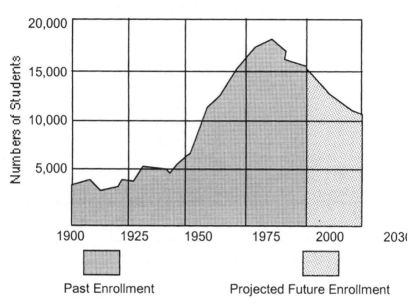

Past Enrollment   Projected Future Enrollment

However, the actual exercise of power and channels of communication often deviate from the official ones as a result of the personalities and talents of the individuals in those positions. Problems within an organization are often the result of the discrepancy between a person's official assignment and that individual's ability to perform the tasks associated with the position. The school-newspaper research project included attention to such discrepancies.

Organization charts are typically accompanied by an explanation of the various positions in the chart and their relationships. The school-newspaper study included the following definitions of the positions identified in Figure 7-6.

The high-school principal is ultimately held responsible for whatever occurs in the school, including the conduct of the school newspaper. Therefore, the principal holds the final power of decision about who serves on the paper and about what sort of content should be allowed in the paper. However, in the daily operation of the paper, this power has been delegated to the faculty sponsor—the teacher in charge of the school's journalism classes.

Figure 7-6

Chart of the Organization of a High School Newspaper Staff

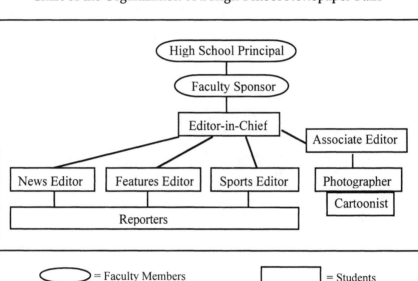

The faculty sponsor (a) trains students in journalism practice, (b) appoints students to their positions, and (b) advises the editors about their responsibilities and about problems they face.

The editor-in-chief (a) confers with the section editors about which stories to include and about which reporters to assign, (b) attempts to resolve conflicts among staff members, (c) writes an editorial for each of the biweekly issues of the paper or assigns someone else to write it, and (d) edits the "letters to the editor" portion of the opinion-and-editorials page.

The associate editor is responsible for (a) the paper's layout (deciding which articles go where), (b) writing headlines, (c) proofreading the final versions of articles, (d) giving assignments to the photographer and cartoonist, and (e) communicating with the printshop that prints the paper.

The section editors (news, features, sports) (a) suggest the types of articles to include in upcoming issues of the paper, (b) assign reporters to write the articles, (c) copyedit the reporters' articles (make corrections, alter the style to render an article more interesting and easier to understand), and (d) submit the articles to the editor-in-chief and associate editor.

The reporters (a) accept assignments from the editors, (b) search out news and features on their own volition and submit the results to their editors, and (c) write the articles.

The photographer and cartoonist (a) receive assignments from the section editors, via the associate editor, and (b) suggest to the editors the types of photos and cartoons that might be of interest to the paper's readers.

Flow Charts

The step-by-step operation of some aspect of education can be summarized in the form of a flow chart or process chart. Figures 7-7 and 7-8 illustrate one common type of flow chart, an example drawn from a study of a junior high school's approach to aiding troubled students.

The purpose of the project was to answer three questions:

1. What is the school's system for helping students who suffer academic, health, social, or behavioral difficulties that teachers feel unable to solve on their own in the typical classroom setting?
2. How satisfactory is the present system? In others words, what problems are there with the traditional system?
3. What changes, if any, could profitably be made in the system?

The researcher summarized the answers to the first and third questions by means of the flow charts in Figures 7-7 and 7-8.

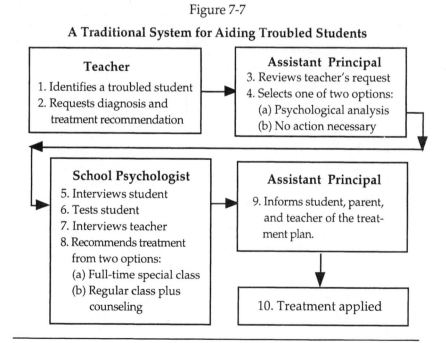

Figure 7-7

A Traditional System for Aiding Troubled Students

Figure 7-8

A Proposed System for Aiding Troubled Students

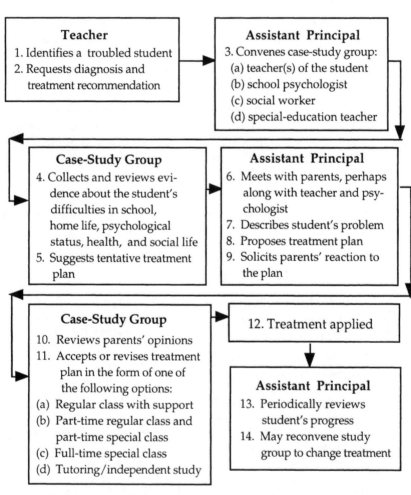

As the contrast between the two figures implies, the evidence gathered to answer the second question suggested that, in the school's traditional approach, (a) not enough knowledgeable people took part in diagnosing the likely causes of a student's difficulties or in suggesting treatment options, (b) a student's parents were not adequately informed of the proposed treatment nor actively engaged in determining the nature of the treatment, (c) too few treatment options were available, and (d) the present approach failed to provide a systematic follow-up assessment of the treatment's success.   Figure 7-8 displays the process that the researcher proposed as a reasonable way of correcting those problems.

Maps

Maps offer readers an instant impression of the locations of places and events.   More precisely, maps are helpful in explaining such matters as transportation routes to schools, the places from which a sample of people were drawn for a survey or an experiment, the effect of population concentration on the location of educational facilities, the historical development of different kinds of schools, and the boundaries of various educational authorities' jurisdiction.   Maps also aid in portraying relationships between a school's curriculum content and the school's surrounding distribution of languages, religions, vocational opportunities, and social-class structures.   Maps are useful as well in providing space comparisons of limited scope—floor-plan designs for a new school, ways of arranging tables and desks in a classroom, the layout of equipment in an auto shop or home-economics laboratory, and alternative traffic patterns for moving students efficiently between class periods.

The ability of maps to offer readers a concise visual summary is illustrated in Figure 7-9, which was created with drawing software on the researcher's laptop computer.   The map of the neighborhood around an elementary school accompanied a research report titled *Coping with Unsafe Places*.   The dual aim of the project was (a) to identify locations near the school that posed dangers for children as they were going to and from school and (b) to suggest ways that those dangers might be reduced or eliminated.   The research focused on four kinds of threats to pupils' safety: (a) accidents that caused physical or emotional injury, (b) physical conflicts (fights) resulting in harm that required medical treatment (school nurse, doctor, hospital), (c) the ingestion of harmful substances (tobacco, alcohol, illicit drugs), and (d) sexual abuse (actual or potential).

The source of data for the report was a collection the past three years' records of incidents focusing on the four kinds of threats.   The numbers on the map identify the 10 most frequent locations of safety hazards.   The map was accompanied by the following description of the numbered sites.

1. *School Playground.*   The largest number of accidents and fights have occurred on the playground during recess, during the lunch hour, before school, after school, and during physical-education periods.   The most common sources of accidents have been the swings, monkey bars, and children falling during running games.   Fights have broken out mainly when no staff member was present or nearby.   Over a three–year period, dozens of playground accidents and fights have been reported.

Figure 7-9

Map of Unsafe Places Near an Elementary School

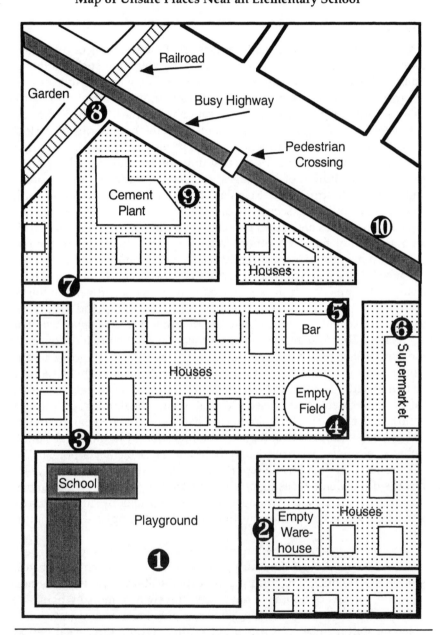

2. *Empty Warehouse.* The abandoned warehouse across Benson Street from the school has been used occasionally by upper-grade pupils as a place to smoke tobacco and marijuana, drink alcohol, and engage in sex play. A total of nine such incidents have been reported. Rumors among the pupils suggest that the actual number of occasions has been considerably greater.

3. *Street Crossing.* Fourteen injuries to children have occurred in front of the school entrance at the juncture of West Clauson Street and Lander Lane. Before school in the morning and at dismissal time in the afternoon, the auto traffic is high at this location, as parents drop off or pick up their children. Most injuries at this spot have happened when a driver did not see a child dart out from behind a car. Thus, either the driver's auto hit the child or the child crashed into the auto.

4. *Empty field.* Children sometimes stop to play in this field on the way home from school. During their play, they occasionally suffer accidents or get into fights. This is also a place where a bully or a gang may waylay a victim and cause either physical or emotional harm.

5. *Bar.* Children passing this bar after school (and particularly upper-grade girls) have occasionally been bothered by men who have been drinking there. The men have made sexually suggestive remarks to the pupils or, on two occasions, offered pupils a drink or a "happy pill" or "happy smoke." According to the police, the bar is suspected of being a place in which illicit drugs are sometimes peddled.

6. *Supermarket Parking Lot.* On several occasions before or after school, pupils have suffered injuries while skateboarding or rollerblading in the parking lot. The supermarket manager has phoned the school to ask that the pupils be prevented from using the parking lot as a playground.

7. *Dangerous Intersection.* Several accidents between autos and pupils on bicycles have happened where West Freemont intersects Lander Lane. Traffic on West Freemont flows rather fast, and tall bushes at the corners obstruct a clear view of the cross street for cyclists who are coming from Lander Lane.

8. *Railroad Trestle.* At the juncture of the railroad and Sheraton Highway, several boys in recent years, while on their way home from school, have been rather seriously injured while playing on the railroad trestle.

9. *Cement Plant.* Children have occasionally been hurt while playing on equipment (tractors, trucks, trailers) parked behind the cement plant.

10. *Highway.* On five occasions, pupils trying to cross Sheraton Highway were either hit by autos or narrowly missed. There is a proper pedestrian crossing at the end of Slade Street, but children who don't want to bother walking to that crossing may try to cross at location 10. Apparently some of the more daring individuals enjoy the challenge of running across in traffic, probably in an effort to show off in front of their classmates.

In sum, the map, accompanied by a brief explanation of the numbered locations, serves as an efficient way to convey the gist of the safety threats and to guide readers through the research report's detailed description of the hazards and of the suggestions for dealing with those threats.

Planning Guide

The following activities offer an opportunity for readers to apply the concepts of this chapter to potential research studies.

1. For a research project that you might wish to carry out:

- State the questions or questions that the study is intended to answer.
- Tell what kinds of information you will need to collect in order to answer the questions, identify the sources of that information, and explain how it would be gathered.
- Describe the classification scheme you would create for organizing the collected information. That is, describe the kinds of categories into which the data would be divided.

2. To answer each of the following questions, describe (a) what kinds of data should be collected and (b) the categories into which those data should be classified.

- What recreational activities are pursued by children ages 5, 8, and 11; how do the activities in which girls engage compare with those in which boys engage; and what are the different levels of complexity of the various activities?

- Does the quality of high school students' written compositions differ when they compose the compositions with a word-processing program rather than writing the compositions by hand?

3. When conducting research to answer each of the following questions, what kinds of statistics, if any, would you include in each report? In each case, why would you use such statistics rather than some other kinds? Or why would you not use any statistics at all?

- During free-play time in a kindergarten, in how many kinds of activities do different children engage and how long do individuals maintain their interest in each kind?

- The positions on the council of a high school's student-body government include president, vice-president, corresponding secretary, recording secretary, treasurer, and two representatives from each of the three class levels in the school—sophomore, junior, and senior. The council is under the supervision of a faculty member. A research project is conducted to answer this question: During a typical meeting of the council, what is the pattern of members' participation in terms of (a) who contributes ideas,

(b) who appears to influence other members' opinions, and (c) by what means is that apparent influence exerted?

- Among the upper-grade pupils of an elementary school, how likely will the children who are most physically fit also be the ones with the best academic performance?

4. If you carried out Activity 1 above, then describe any tables or graphs that you would include in your research plan. If you intend to have one or more tables, identify the form of each table by indicating which variables would be placed on the horizontal and vertical axes. In other words, prepare *dummy tables*—ones in which the cells within the body of the tables are empty. If you would intend to include one or more graphic displays, draw a sketch of each graph, chart, or map and label its parts.

8

Interpreting the Outcomes

One way to view research is in terms of two phases—description and interpretation. In the descriptive phase, the researcher is responsible for accurately depicting the events and people that are the objects of the research. In the interpretive stage, the researcher proposes meanings that go beyond the description itself. Whereas the descriptive stage tells what happened, the interpretive stage suggests what the happenings mean. Thus, different investigators—using the same description of events—can produce quite different research reports by assigning different meanings to the data. The purpose of this chapter is to illustrate how that can occur. The presentation consists of identifying various kinds of meaning that can be attributed to descriptive material by offering examples of how teachers might devise each of those kinds of meaning.

The types of interpretation addressed in the following pages are labeled (a) status, (b) causation, (c) comparison, (d) evaluation, (e) extension, and (f) prediction. Three subtypes under causation concern function, process, and context.

As the discussion of types advances, it will become apparent that the clue to which type of meaning is involved in a given project is found in the way the research question is worded. Here are five examples in which the type of interpretation implied in a research question is indicated in the parentheses at the end of the question.

- What consequences for teachers resulted from the school district's adopting the *assertive discipline* program? (causation)
- What sequence of steps was followed in determining the amount of funds to be allocated to teachers for buying instructional supplies? (process)
- How likely is it that the pattern of test results for inner-city fourth-graders is true as well for fourth-graders in the suburban school districts outside the city? (extension)

- What instructional role can computers be expected to play in classrooms 10 years from now? (prediction)
- What influence did the shooting at Livermore High have on the sense of security of students at both Livermore High and at the district's other three secondary schools? (context)

As these queries suggest, although the task of providing an interpretation comes near the end of a research project—after the data have been collected and organized— the kind of interpretation the researcher hopes to draw is typically implied at the outset of the study in the project's target questions.

Status

When the entire purpose of a research project is to depict the status or condition of an educational phenomenon, then no interpretation beyond the descriptive information is needed. In other words, the "meaning" of the study is the descriptive information itself. The status of interest can be either in the present or in the past, as illustrated by such guide questions as:

- Which television programs do our middle-school students watch and how frequently do they watch each type?
- What kinds of humor are published in the city's high-school newspapers?
- What types of classes, as shown by their titles and descriptions, were offered in our high school in 1950?
- How much time do fifth-grade students spend doing homework in each subject-matter field during a typical month?
- Which people were most influential in affecting the educational career of Mrs. Julia Wentworth, who recently retired as principal of Jefferson High School?

Causation

Every proposal about causes assumes that two or more events or variables are correlated. This is the assumption that whenever something happens to one of the correlated variables, something will also happen to the others. When atmospheric temperature descends from plus-20 degrees to minus-20 degrees Centigrade, water will turn into ice; so people are prone to conclude that the drop in temperature *caused* the change in the water. When a teenager joins a street gang and thereafter smokes marijuana and engages in street fights, observers are apt to propose that the cause of the youth's errant behavior has been his delinquent companions. Ergo, if the lad had chosen law-abiding companions, he would not now be smoking and fighting.

As explained in Chapter 5, establishing that two or more variables are correlated is not sufficient for arguing that one variable is the cause of the other. Assigning a cause-and-effect meaning to a research project's results requires not only evidence of correlation but also a line of logic that convinces readers that one of the variables was, indeed, responsible—at least partially—for why another variable behaved as it did. Consider, for example, five modes of reasoning about (a) time sequence, (b) withdrawal/return, (c) consistency, (d) combined variables, and (e) influential conditions.

A time-sequence argument holds that one of the correlated events or variables (the cause) occurred before the other (the effect), and that the two events could not have happened in reverse order. The time-sequence rationale is easiest to support whenever Variable A has been operating at a steady state for some time before Variable B appears. Upon the arrival of Variable B, the condition of Variable A changes and continues its changed status as long as Variable B is present. As an obvious example, a third-grade boy is a continual problem for his teacher because the boy is constantly on the move—wiggling, chattering, bothering his neighbors, walking about the classroom, and not completing his assignments. A school psychologist observes the boy and proposes that he exhibits an attention-deficit disorder accompanied by hyperactivity. The pupil is placed on medication, and his behavior changes so that he is no longer restless or bothersome, and he can concentrate on his studies. Thus, the medication (Variable B) is judged to be the cause of the change in the hyperactivity (Variable A). In effect, it is reasonable to believe that administering the medication preceded the cessation of hyperactivity and not vice versa.

The argument that Variable B is the cause of Variable A is further strengthened if, when B is removed, A reverts to its pre-B state. So, if the third-grader stops taking his medication and once more turns hyperactive and distractible, the notion that the medication had been the cause of the boy's more placid demeanor is increasingly convincing. The argument becomes even more persuasive if the medication is then reinstated and the hyperactivity once again declines.

A causation rationale can also be buttressed by evidence that the postulated cause-effect pattern has occurred many times without exception (or with rare exception). By way of illustration, consider a debate over the influence of homework on students' school achievement. Teachers who agree that assigning homework leads to greater achievement can still disagree about whether it is important for a teacher to grade homework assignments and then require students to correct any weaknesses found. Imagine, now, that a researcher investigates this issue by studying 30 classrooms in which math homework is assigned. In 15 classes, students get credit for handing in their assignments, but they receive no feedback from the teacher about how adequate their work has been. In the other 15 classes, how much credit students receive depends on the quality of their homework, as judged by the teacher, and on how satisfactorily the students then remedy shortcomings the teacher has identified. Let's also imagine that, after the two patterns of treating homework in the 30 classes has been applied for several weeks, (a) the quality of students' performance on homework assignments and in-class tests is assessed and (b) the improvement scores for each of the 15 feedback classes are considerably higher than those for each of the 15 no-feedback classes. This sort of evidence, showing a consistent effect across classes, supports the proposal that feedback (Variable B) affects performance (Variable A).

Rarely—probably never—is any event the result of a single causal element. Hence, an effort to find *the sole cause* is likely futile. The best a researcher can hope for is to identify the most powerful factor or factors among the combination of components that appear to determine an educational outcome of interest—such an outcome as reading skill. Changing that factor might be enough to produce some degree of improvement in the outcome.

The task of identifying the most influential factors involves two steps: (a) measuring or estimating the degree of correlation between various factors and the educational outcome and (b) adducing a persuasive line of reasoning that an identified factor was at least a partial cause of the outcome and not simply a coincidental correlate of the outcome. For instance, in a massive international research project focusing on pupils' reading skills in 26 nations, the correlation coefficients between (a) various factors (indicators) and (b) reading skill showed that

> the two indicators where there are important differences in many countries between the most effective and least effective schools are the frequency of [pupils] borrowing books from a library and voluntary reading. Whether these indicators reflect home environments or whether there is more encouragement for these activities in more effective schools is not known. However, both the borrowing of books from libraries and reading for pleasure can be encouraged by teachers. (Postlethwaite & Ross, 1992, p. 27)

Thus, the correlation between reading skill and the two variables (book borrowing, voluntary reading) was noteworthy. However, the researchers did not have enough evidence about pupils' home conditions (parents' own reading habits, parents encouraging their children to read, numbers and kinds of reading materials in the home) to judge how much of the influence on children's reading abilities likely came from the home in comparison to the influence of the school or children's companions. But, in order to draw some practical guidance from the research results, the researchers were willing to suggest, on the basis of their correlation evidence, that one reasonable step toward improve reading would be for teachers to encourage book borrowing and leisure-time reading.

One of the complicating features in the search for cause is the fact that the correlation between one variable (frequency of homework) and another (reading skill) will be affected by conditions that can differ from one case to another. Therefore, researchers are obliged to qualify their conclusions in a manner that recognizes the conditional relationship between the variables. Sometimes the influential conditions can be identified, or at least estimated. Other times they are unknown. An identified or estimated condition is reflected in such an observation as "Math scores were higher for pupils whose parents supervised their children's homework assignments," where the influential condition was parental supervision. In contrast, an example of researchers recognizing the existence of influential conditions, but not being able to specify the nature of those conditions, is found in a comment by the authors of the reading report.

> Students in more effective schools spend more time on homework than in less effective schools but, although this is one of the more important indicators in Canada, Hungary, and New Zealand, the difference [between more and less effective schools] is not great. (Postlethwaite & Ross, 1992, p. 27)

In effect, certain conditions distinguished Canada, Hungary, and New Zealand from the other 23 nations in the study, but the evidence the authors had available did not reveal what those conditions might be.

Cause Subtypes

Researchers sometimes find it convenient to focus their interpretations on subtypes of the causation explanation. Three such subtypes concern *function, process,* and *context.*

A function interpretation is an estimate of the role played by individuals, groups, institutions, or events in producing a particular result. Function is implied in such research questions as the following.

- What part do teachers play in determining the content and form of test items on the standardized tests used in elementary schools throughout the county?
- What strategies are used by lobbyists for publishing companies to influence the school district's purchase of textbooks, and how effective are those strategies?
- In the city's five high schools, how closely does the formal job description for the position of *Assistant Principal for Student Affairs* match what the person in that position actually does day by day? How can mismatches between the formal job definition and the incumbent's daily activities be explained?

Process interpretations are proposals about the sequence of events that contribute to some outcome of interest.

- At what junctures in a teacher's relationship with students can teachers most effectively cope with students who harass classmates?
- What is our school's current system for procuring and using computer software for classroom instruction, and how could that system be made more efficient?
- By what means can primary-grade teachers identify pupils who likely suffer visual-perception difficulties?

Context interpretations are estimates of how the overall combination of factors that compose a setting in which an event occurs influence the consequences of the event, that is, influence the consequences experienced by people and institutions.

- In what ways does placing a disabled learner (one with markedly below average learning aptitude) in a regular sixth-grade classroom affect that learner and the other pupils in the class?
- How does the arrangement of classroom furniture and of wall displays (bulletin boards, chalkboards, window decorations) affect how well students focus on their learning assignments (how well students attend to the teacher's instruction, how often students disturb their classmates, how much they daydream, and the like)?
- How are routine classroom activities (the activities usually pursued) influenced by unusual events in the surrounding society, and how might the routines be altered so as to accommodate such influence in a constructive way? The term *unusual events* refers to such happenings as the outbreak of war, a street riot, an auto accident in which students or members of their family die, or the kidnapping of a fellow student.

Summary

For the purpose of improving the conduct of schooling, the most helpful way of interpreting a study's outcomes is often that of assigning causal meaning to the research results. However, because of the complex nature of the causes of events, responsible researchers are obliged to (a) take great care in collecting information, (b) recognize that multiple variables or factors contribute to any outcome, (c) calculate or estimate the degree of correlation among variables, and (d) build a line of logic that distinguishes causal relationships from coincidental relationships.

Comparisons

Assigning meaning to data from the vantage point of comparison consists of showing how something is similar to and different from something else. The word *compare* is sometimes used to mean identifying likenesses between two or more things, whereas *contrast* is used to mean identifying ways things differ from each other. However, in the following discussion, the word *compare* refers to citing both likenesses and differences among phenomena. A typical assumption behind adopting comparison as the perspective from which to understand things is that the greater the number of ways two or more things are seen as being alike and different, the more meaningful those things become.

One useful way to analyze comparisons is in terms of (a) the entities that are being compared, (b) characteristics of those entities that are the focus of the comparison, and (c) the units of comparison (Table 8-1).

Comparisons can consist solely of qualitative characteristics (likenesses and difference in *kind*) or can include quantitative evidence (likenesses and differences in *amount* or *magnitude*). For example, consider a qualitative narrative comparing twin sisters who achieved prominence in high school. The characteristics in the comparison focuses include age, physical appearance, academic record, interests, and social relationships.

On graduation day, Doris and Dana Merton capped off their illustrious high-school careers by being selected as co-valedictorians. These two handsome 17-year-olds were identical twins, who not only looked alike but usually dressed alike, so even close friends had difficulty telling the two apart unless the twins were engaged in their favorite activities. Doris's intense interest in science and mathematics was reflected in the elective classes she chose in high school and in the advanced courses she was permitted to take in the community college. Music was Dana's area of specialization. She was an accomplished vocalist and a master of stringed instruments, qualified to play cello in the city symphony orchestra and to play guitar in a girls' band that performed at school dances and assembly programs. The twins' wide-ranging talents and strong competitive spirit equipped them to earn straight-A academic records in high school. Doris was the friendlier of the two, more inclined than her sister to initiate contact with a wide variety of classmates, a trait that contributed to Doris's election as president of the senior class. Dana, in contrast, limited her socializing to a few close friends, all of them musicians.

Next, consider a typical quantitative comparison, showing the results of sixth-graders' success on the 100-point Wentworth Reading Test in five elementary schools

Oak	Washington	Monarch	Central	Westview
n=63	n=72	n=81	n=57	n=44
M=53.7	M=64.6	M=43.1	M=48.9	M=68.8
Mdn=54	Mdn=58	Mdn=45	Mdn=49	Mdn=62
SD=6.7	SD=7.1	SD=6.8	SD=8.3	SD=5.9

Code: n=number of pupils   M=mean   Mdn= median   SD=standard deviation

Table 8-1

Components of Comparisons

The Compared Entities	The Compared Characteristics	The Units of Comparison
Boys and girls	Height at ages 4, 7, 10, 13, 16	Feet and inches
Four high school science textbooks	Factual accuracy	Science facts
	Quality of writing	How well students understand a text
	Informative illustrations	Photos, diagrams
	Cost	Dollars
	Up-to-date	Recent science issues and theories
Five elementary schools	Quality of buildings	Size, age, condition
	Budgeted income	Dollars
	Size of teaching faculty	Pupils per teacher
	Quality of personnel	% credentialed staff
Three high schools	Use of discretionary funds	The particular items and services bought
Thirty parents of fifth-graders	Parents' attitudes about pupils' schooling	Parents' answers to teacher's questions
Four school psychologists	Methods of diagnosing pupil behavior problems	Steps in the diagnosis process
All students in a junior high school	School rule infractions	Incidence of breaking each type of rule
Twenty-seven high school students	English-language vocabulary	Accurate definitions of words
Pupils in special-education class	Frequency of school attendance	Number of days absent from school

The statistics in the comparison of pupils scores on the Wentworth reading exam are accompanied by the following narrative interpretation.

Westview's sixth-graders, with an average score of 68.8, were the most effective readers among the pupils in the five schools. Washington pupils, at 64.6, were a close second. Sixth-graders at Monarch were the least skilled readers, with a mean of 43.1 that was nearly 26 points below the Westview average. Pupils' scores were spread out most at Central (standard deviation of 8.3) and bunched together most at Westview (standard deviation 5.9). That the scores were most evenly divided above and below the middle of the distributions at Central and Oak (resulting in apparent bell-shaped "normal" distributions) is suggested by the fact that in those two schools the mean and median were nearly identical. In contrast, the difference between the mean and median in Washington (6.6-points difference) and Westview (6.8-points difference) indicates that those distributions were skewed toward the lower end of the scale (that is, scores above the middle were more bunched together, and those below the middle were more strung out).

When researchers seek to convey to their readers what some potentially puzzling feature of their research means, they may compare the feature to something with which readers are already familiar, showing how that feature is in some ways like, and in some ways different from, the something that readers already understand. In other words, researchers often depend on analogies to clarify their meanings. Here are three examples.

Inertia theory. Among Sir Isaac Newton's contributions to physical science are his three laws of motion. The first of these postulates—the law of inertia—asserts that a body at rest or moving at a constant speed in a straight line will remain at rest or will continue moving in a straight line at constant speed unless acted upon by a force. In the following pages, I propose that the concept of inertia can profitably be transferred from the field of physics into the social sciences as a perspective from which to interpret cases of planned social change, including the sort of change known as educational development, educational reform, or educational innovation. In effect, inertia in an education system is the complex force that resists change—that fosters "business as usual." (Thomas, 2002, p. 3).

Organizational structure. The authority structure of a typical school district is in many ways similar to the authority structure of an army. The top-level authority for the U.S. military consists of the U.S. president and Congress, who establish policies governing the conduct of military affairs but do not directly participate in those affairs. In a similar manner, the top-level authority for a school district consists of the president of the school board and the school-board members, who set policy for the operation of the schools but do not play a direct role in schooling activities. In the military, within the body of professional soldiers, there is a pyramid-shaped hierarchy of authority extending from generals at the top through descending levels of officers to arrive at the ranks of the enlisted personnel who carry out orders from above. Likewise, in a school district, within the body of professional educators, there is pyramid-shaped hierarchy of authority extending from the superintendent of schools at the top through descending levels of administrators to arrive at the ranks of teachers who do the actual work of educating students.

Diagnostic teaching. The instructional approach known as *diagnostic teaching* can be likened to diagnosis and treatment process in medical practice. A physician, at the diagnostic stage, examines the patient to identify the strengths and weaknesses of the patient's physical and mental health. Then, for whatever faults the diagnosis reveals, the physician (a) estimates the causes of those faults and (b) prescribes specific treatments (medication, surgery, physical therapy, diet) to correct the deficiencies. Diagnostic teaching follows this same pattern. A teacher, rather than beginning by offering a student instruction (lectures, textbook readings, videotapes), starts by examining the student's knowledge (tests, interviews) to identify strengths and weaknesses in what the student knows. Then, for whatever inadequacies the diagnosis exposes, the teacher (a) estimates the causes and (b) prescribes specific treatments (reading materials, tutoring, improved diet, a change of companions, more sleep, etc.) to remedy the shortcomings.

Evaluation

Evaluation is a particular kind of comparison whose nature can be explained by distinguishing between *facts* and *values*. The term *facts,* as typically intended, refers to observations or measurements that are publicly verifiable. In contrast, *values* are statements about the desirability or propriety or goodness of something. The "something" may be a person, an object, a place, an event, an idea, a kind of behavior, a teaching method, an administrative decision, or the like.

All of the comparisons in Table 8-1 (page 168) are factual. Each calls for only a description of children's heights, of school buildings, of psychologists' diagnostic methods, and such. None calls for opinions about whether one child's height or one building or one diagnostic technique is better than another. One the other hand, our earlier description of twins Doris and Dana is a mixture of facts and values (evaluations), with some of the values implied rather than stated outright. Examples of factual information are the girl's ages, their grades in school, and their special interests as reflected in their activities. But the words *handsome, friendlier,* and *accomplished-vocalist* are value judgments—reflections of opinions about better and worse. Likewise, the notion that the twins were academically superior to most of their schoolmates is implied in the report that they were *co-valedictorians* and had *straight-A records.* Furthermore, Doris's enrolling in college courses and Dana's playing cello in the city symphony also imply an evaluation—an opinion about the girls' superiority.

The report of sixth-graders' reading-test scores is similarly a mixture of facts and values. Whereas the statistics are factual, readers are likely to draw value interpretations by inferring that higher reading scores are better than lower ones. But whether a person would also infer values from the standard deviations (which express the extent of variability among a group's scores) depends on whether that person believes it is better to have the reading abilities of pupils in a class be much alike (bunched together) or, in contrast, thinks it is better for scores to be diverse (spread over a wide range).

My purpose for drawing the distinction between factual comparisons and value comparisons (evaluations) is twofold. First, I believe it is important for researchers to decide whether the interpretations they derive from their data should offer only factual comparisons or should include value judgments. Second, if the interpretations are to contain value judgments (evaluations), then it is important for readers to recognize the standards on which those judgments are based. This question of standards is the matter to which we now turn.

The essence of the standards issue is expressed in Mrs. Jones's response to Mrs. Smith when Mrs. Smith inquired, "How's your husband?" And Mrs. Jones responded, "Compared to what?" In effect, every evaluation involves matching something—such as a husband—against a standard or criterion. It's important for readers of a research report to know what the intended standard is.

One way that evaluation standards can differ is in their specificity, as illustrated in the following three evaluations of a student's autobiographical sketch. Teacher A's assessment reflected the least specific standard, whereas Teacher C's judgment reflected the most specific criterion. A similar characteristic of standards illustrated in the three examples is explicitness—the extent to which the teachers' criteria are directly described rather than left to the reader's imagination.

Teacher A: Matthew's autobiography was not very well written.

Teacher B: Matthew had some interesting experiences to describe, and his general writing style was not bad, but he has a lot of work to do on the mechanics of writing.

Teachr C: My evaluation of Matthew's autobiography showed that he (1) described important events in his life (2) in an understandable order but, in doing so, he
(3) misspelled nine words,
(4) committed five comma-splice errors (he hooked together independent sentences with commas),
(5) used "who" when he should have used "whom," and
(6) ended abruptly without a conclusion or summary.

In summary, evaluative interpretations in research reports are most effective when the standards on which the evaluations are based are specific and clearly identified.

Extension

The overview of survey methods in Chapter 5 drew a distinction between *descriptive* conclusions and *inferential* conclusions that are derived from research data. A descriptive conclusion is intended to apply solely to the people, institutions, or events that were directly studied. In contrast, an inferential conclusion extends beyond the immediate participants in a research project to encompass people, institutions, or events that were not directly investigated. Inferential interpretations assume that information about the studied entity – the *sample* – applies equally well to a broader collection of entities – the *population*.

Two techniques were suggested in Chapter 5 for estimating how reasonable it is to extend interpretations to include entities not studied. The first technique involved statistical estimates of the probability of making an error in proposing such an extension. But whether such a technique is appropriate depends on the sample's relationship to the population, that is, on how the sample was drawn – randomly, systematically, or simply by convenience. The second technique – the one to which researchers may turn when they have a convenience sample – involves arguing that the apparent causal factors operating in the sample are the same factors that are working in the larger population. One or both of these techniques is required to support a researcher's (a) interpreting conclusions about entities directly studied as (b) being applicable also to other entities not studied.

Prediction

Interpretation in the form of prediction consists of estimating what is likely to occur in the future as projected from the analysis of past and present trends. Predicting is a form of causation interpretation, since speculating about what will likely occur in times ahead is founded on estimates of (a) what factors have caused matters to arrive at their present state and (b) how those factors will probably influence future events.

To illustrate one common way a predictive study can be conducted, we can use the situation portrayed earlier in the trend graph on page 151. The research question is: How many students will likely be in the school district's elementary and secondary schools in 2030?

We begin by assuming that school-age children come from relatively young families, that is, families in which the parents are mainly between ages 20 and 40. If we can estimate the rate at which such families will enter and leave the community over the next two decades, we can offer a prediction of the size of the school population in 2030. Thus, as a second step, we speculate about which factors significantly affect the number of young families that will be in the community at any given time. Our speculating produces four factors that we regard as particularly salient—cost of living, affordable housing, employment opportunities, and the school system's reputation.

Our third step consists of gathering information about each of the four factors as they existed in the recent past, such as in 1983, 1988, 1993, 1998, and 2003, as well as in earlier times (1900, 1925, 1950, 1975). The expression *cost of living* means a typical family's outlay for daily goods and services. *Affordable housing* refers to the availability of residences (rented or purchased) that fit a family's income. *Employment opportunities* refers to the access families have to jobs, either within the school district or within reasonable commuting distance, that suit parents' skills and interests and that pay wages sufficient for the cost of living and affordable housing. Finally, in choosing a community in which to settle, some parents consider the quality of the schools their children will attend. Thus, a school system's reputation is a fourth factor affecting our prediction.

To collect evidence about the four factors in the past, we can turn to the local Chamber of Commerce, county records, and newspaper archives that perhaps can be found on the World Wide Web.

With the collected data in hand, we can plot the trends of each factor over the past two decades and then project those trends into the future. Principles that guide our prediction are summarized in Table 8-2 on page 174. Finally, the summarized trend for the future can be described in a narrative and depicted in the form of the trend graph on page 151.

The following are additional research questions that call for prediction interpretations.

- In another 20 years, what will be the ethnic composition of the school district's student population in terms of (a) which ethnic groups are included and (b) the quantity of students in each group?

- Unless serious remedies are adopted, what will be the incidence of bullying in local schools 15 years from now?

- How accurately does the *Basic Social Skills Inventory*, administered to seventh-graders, predict those students' popularity with their peers by the time they are high-school seniors?

- In view of the recent policy changes in the allocation of tax moneys to public schools, what amount of funds will likely be available to the district's elementary schools over the next decade?

Table 8-2

Principles to Guide School Enrollment Predictions

Enrollments rise when:	*Enrollments decline when:*
1. The cost of living is well within families' ability to pay.	The cost of living seriously strains families' incomes.
2. There is a larger supply of houses than there is a demand for houses, so competition among sellers drives house prices down.	The supply of houses is insufficient to meet the demand, so competition among buyers drives house prices up.
3. There is a high demand for workers in the region, so applicants can easily find well-paying jobs.	There is an oversupply of qualified workers in the community, so it is difficult to find a job, and pay levels are low.
4. Schools have an excellent reputation in terms of published test scores, honors, graduation rates, variety of services, and lack of disorder.	Schools have a poor reputation in terms of published test scores, dropout rates, drug use, violence, and disorder.

Planning Guide

1. *Interpretation types.* For practice in distinguishing among types of interpretation that are implied by different research questions, in the blank in front of each of the following questions insert the code letter of the type of interpretation that you think the question calls for.

Code letters
A = Status or Condition
B = Causation (function, process, context)
C = Comparison
D = Evaluation
E = Extension
F = Prediction

If you believe a question implies more than one type of interpretation, insert each appropriate code letter in the blank.

_____Which instructional method—textbook assignments or teacher lectures—leads to more effective learning for most students in a high-school American history class?

_____In what ways do parents' reading habits affect what elementary-school students read, how often, and how well?

____What can a survey of 1,500 high-school students' alcohol-drinking habits tell us about the drinking habits of our state's population of high-school students?

____In their knowledge of earth science, how similar were boys and girls in the school's four eighth-grade general-science classes at the end of the school year?

____What variety of discipline techniques are employed by the junior-high-school's teachers, and for what sorts of infractions is each kind of technique used?

____What responsibilities do teachers' aides assume in different nursery schools, and how can the likenesses and differences between aides' tasks in different schools be explained?

____What changes can be expected in teacher-credentialing requirements during the upcoming state-legislature session?

____In a high-school art class, how do the students rank in terms of artistic creativity?

2. *Causation.* Carry out the following activities for a research study you might wish to conduct for identifying the likely causes of the phenomenon on which your study focuses.

(a) State the question—or questions—the study is expected to answer.

(b) Describe the kinds of information you will need to answer the question, and tell why those kinds of information should equip you to furnish a convincing answer.

(c) Suggest the sources from which you might obtain the needed information, and describe the methods you might use for collecting such data.

3. *Comparison.* In a research project you might conduct for comparing two or more phenomena, carry out steps (a), (b), and (c) that are listed under activity 2 above.

4. *Evaluation.* For a study you might wish to conduct for evaluating some educational phenomenon, carry out steps (a), (b), and (c) that are listed under activity 2.

5. *Extension.* Carry out steps (a), (b), and (c) for a study that you might conduct in which you wish to apply to a larger population the conclusions that you would draw from a sample that you directly investigated.

9

Reporting the Results

Chapter 1 identified 13 channels through which reports of research might be disseminated to a variety of interested audiences:

A teacher's oral presentation at a faculty meeting
An article in a school newspaper
An item in a newsletter distributed to members of an education association
A bulletin issued by a school district or a university research bureau
A teacher's master's-degree thesis or doctoral dissertation
A paper delivered at an educational conference
A report at a university seminar
An item in a daily newspaper or weekly news magazine
An item on a radio or television news hour
An article in a professional journal
An entry on an Internet website
A chapter in a book
An entire book

The purpose of the present chapter is to describe in some detail how teachers can take advantage of those channels for publishing the results of their own research. The chapter is divided into six sections titled (a) oral presentations, (b) popular periodicals, (c) theses and dissertations, (d) journals and bulletins, (e) the Internet, and (f) books and book chapters. Each section focuses on four issues: (a) the research report's intended audience, (b) an appropriate writing style, (c) how to submit a report, and (d) advantages and disadvantages of that method of publishing research outcomes.

Oral Presentations

Appropriate occasions for oral reports of research include school faculty meetings, Parent-Teacher-Association nights, service-club luncheons (Rotary, Kiwanis, Lions, Chamber of Commerce), radio and television newscasts and interview programs, university seminars, and professional-education conferences.

The way outcomes of research are most effectively reported depends to a great extent on the audience for which the report is intended. Therefore, in preparing an oral presentation, the researcher can profitably begin by estimating the interests, background information, and mindset that members of the audience will likely bring to the session. The presentation can then be fashioned to fit those conditions.

For instance, reports intended for the general public (service-club, radio, TV) are most successful when they are relatively brief and when they feature the results of the study, practical applications of the results, a nontechnical description of the methodology used, and any curious incidents that arose during the conduct of the project. Statistics mentioned should be ones with which members of the general public are familiar, such as averages and percentages.

In contrast, descriptions intended for such specialized audiences as those found in university seminars and at professional-education conferences can be more detailed and focus more on problems of methodology and the interpretation of data. References to statistical treatments can meaningfully include such expressions as *standard deviation, ANOVA, t-test,* and *systematic sampling.*

There are several ways to find opportunities to report research orally. If the teacher has conducted the study as part of university graduate work (term project, thesis, dissertation), then the student's faculty advisor can arrange for an in-class or seminar presentation. The chance to report the study at a professional conference can be arranged by submitting a written abstract of the work to the conference program committee. To discover if a service club would like to have the project described at a luncheon session, the teacher can phone or write to the club's program chairman and describe the nature of the project. In a similar fashion, phoning or writing to a news editor at a television or radio station is a useful way to learn if the editor would like to receive a written account of the research or else would want to invite the author to be interviewed on the air.

Compared to other ways of disseminating research results, oral presentations have the advantage of permitting the author to adjust the report to the time constraints of the setting and to embellish the report in response to questions from the audience. Oral reports are also accompanied by potential disadvantages. The time permitted for the presentation may be unexpectedly curtailed, thus preventing the author from explaining all that the audience should hear. Or because of the room's unsatisfactory acoustics or the speaker's faulty enunciation, listeners may not be able to hear the presentation clearly so that they miss important information.

Popular Periodicals

Some studies conducted by teachers are suited for such periodicals as newspapers and magazines aimed at the general public. Articles based on teachers' research are usually short, focusing mainly on the research outcomes and their application in daily life. Any mention of the methodology of the project will be brief and nontechnical.

One way to submit an article to a popular periodical consists of the author printing the article as a *press release* that is sent to a variety of newspapers or magazines. Another way is to phone an editor, describe the nature of the study, and offer to send an account of the work for the editor's consideration.

The main advantage of publishing in a popular periodical is that the author's research reaches a large audience of people from various walks of life. A disadvantage is that, because the report is necessarily brief, readers do not obtain a detailed understanding of the research methodology or outcomes.

Theses and Dissertations

School-focused research is often part of a master's-degree or doctoral program in which a teacher is enrolled. The results of the work become published in the form of a thesis or dissertation available to readers at the library of the institution the teacher has attended. The research reaches a wider audience if the institution publishes a collection of abstracts of the current year's theses and dissertations, a collection that may appear in either printed form or on the institution's Internet website.

An abstract of a dissertation can also be placed on the website entitled *ProQuest Digital Dissertations* (wwwlib.umi.com/dissertations/), which contains more than 1.6 million citations. Both dissertations and theses can also be included in the collection labeled *Dissertation Abstracts Online* (wwwlibrary.dialog.com/bluesheets/html/bl0035.html), which is described as

a definitive subject, title, and author guide to virtually every American dissertation accepted at an accredited institution since 1861. Selected Masters theses have been included since 1962. In addition, since 1988, the database includes citations for dissertations from 50 British universities that have been collected by and filmed at The British Document Supply Centre. Beginning with DAIC Volume 49, Number 2 (Spring 1988), citations and abstracts from Section C, Worldwide Dissertations (formerly European Dissertations), have been included in the file. Abstracts are included for doctoral records from July 1980 (*Dissertation Abstracts International*, Volume 41, Number 1) to the present. Abstracts are included for masters theses from Spring 1988 (*Masters Abstracts*, Volume 26, Number 1) to the present. (*Dissertation Abstracts Online*, 2003).

Information about how authors can have their works included in such collections is available at the central library of the college or university in which the teacher has completed graduate studies.

An important advantage of issuing a research report as a thesis or dissertation is that the length of the report is not restricted. A detailed explanation can be offered describing each step in the project. However, unless the work has been placed on the Internet or a short version has been published as a journal or newspaper article, the distribution of the report is restricted to the people who use the library of the institution in which the author earned the graduate degree.

Journals and Bulletins

Thousands of journals, bulletins, and newsletters publish articles of interest to readers in particular occupations and fields of knowledge. The names of publications that might be appropriate outlets for a teacher's research report can be found on Internet websites and in a library's lists of periodicals to which that library subscribes.

Academic journals can be issued monthly, bimonthly, quarterly, semiannually, or annually. The most common publication schedule is perhaps quarterly. Each journal accepts articles in a defined field of interest:

- An academic discipline, such as *American Anthropologist, Child Development, Journal of Cross-Cultural Psychology,* and *Social Forces*
- A professional specialization, such as *Journal of Correctional Education, Journal of the Association for the Severely Handicapped,* and *The American Music Teacher*
- An ethnic group, such as *American Indian Culture and Research Journal, Bulletin of Hispanic Studies, Journal of Black Studies,* and *Journal of Japanese Studies*
- A gender category, such as *Women's Studies Quarterly* and *Women's Rights Law Reporter*
- A religious denomination, such as *Lutheran Theological Journal, Journal of New Communal Services, Muslim Education Quarterly,* and *U.S. Catholic*

The nature and size of a journal's reading audience are influenced by such conditions as the publication's subject-matter focus, the journal's reputation, its cost, how widely it is advertised, the quality of its articles, and whether it is issued by a professional society. Whenever a journal is the main publication of a professional group or scholarly society, everyone belonging to the organization usually receives the journal by right of membership. Therefore, the larger the society's membership, the larger the reading audience. However, many other journals—not automatically distributed to an organization's members—must depend entirely on paid subscriptions for their distribution. Because subscription prices are frequently high, individuals often avoid buying the journals and depend, instead, on library copies. However, in recent years, as library funds have diminished, many libraries have eliminated subscriptions to journals that are seldom read or are particularly expensive, so the reading audience for such publications has dwindled.

To learn how and where to submit an article to a journal, researchers can inspect copies of the journal or turn to the publication's website on the Internet. Examining copies of the journal informs authors of the format, subject-matter focus, writing style, and length of articles that the publication accepts and the address to which manuscripts should be sent. The journal's website typically provides more detailed information about the rules governing the acceptance and publication of articles.

Journals can differ dramatically in the proportion of submitted articles that they ultimately publish. The most prestigious and popular periodicals may accept as few as 15% of the papers they receive. In contrast, journals of substantially lower status or ones with a small potential audience may publish 80% or more of submitted articles.

The acceptable length of articles can vary from one journal to another. Some editors limit entries to no more than ten printed pages. Others accept reports as long as 40 or 50 pages. Frequently, the periodical's policy regarding length is explained on the journal's inside cover (front or rear) or on the publication's Internet website.

The time lag between an author's submitting a paper to a journal and the paper actually appearing in print can differ markedly from one journal to another. In some cases the time period can be as short as six months. At the other extreme, it can be as long as three or four years.

Journals are not all alike in their policies regarding the costs that authors are expected to bear and the payments authors may receive. Most academic and professional periodicals neither charge authors anything for publishing their articles nor pay authors for their work. However, some require authors to contribute toward the publishing expense (usually a given amount per printed page), whereas others pay writers a modest sum for their work.   Authors usually receive two or three free copies of the issue of the journal in which their paper appears, and they may also be sent 25 or more offprints of their article.

Academic and professional societies, in addition to publishing journals and bulletins, often send newsletters to their members and to libraries. Articles in journals usually consist of detailed, formal accounts of research methods and outcomes, supported liberally with citations from the professional literature.   In contrast, articles in newsletters are typically brief descriptions of research results, frequently written in an informal style without footnotes or references to other studies.   It is often easier to have a newsletter article accepted for publication than a journal article.

There are a number of advantages to publishing in a journal rather than reporting research orally or in a popular periodical.   Journal articles are usually more detailed, explain technical features that are important to specialists in the particular field of interest, and carry greater prestige in academic circles than do oral presentations, newspaper accounts, and magazine articles.   However, authors usually wait a rather long time before their submission to a journal gets into print, and the number of people who read their article will be small if the journal has a limited subscription list.

The Internet

An unprecedented opportunity for researchers to reach a global audience appeared in the closing years of the 20th century with the invention and continuing expansion of the computer Internet and its World Wide Web.   By 2001 there were over 533 million Internet users throughout the world (249 million in the United States, 115 million in the Asia-Pacific region, 126 million in Western Europe, and the remaining 143 million elsewhere).   By 2004 the worldwide total would reach 945 million users, with an estimated growth to 1,460 million by 2007 (Internet Users, 2002).

There are three principal ways that teachers can distribute their research reports via the Internet and World Wide Web.   The simplest way is by e-mail (electronic mail), which operates in much the same fashion as postal mail, except that messages are delivered over the computer network rather than by a postal worker.   An author seated at a computer transmits the report either (a) to particular readers at their network addresses (with the names and e-mail addresses of people interested in the teacher's topic obtained from mailing lists available on the Internet) or (b) to one or more of the thousands of special interest groups found on the Internet, with appropriate interest groups identified and reached by means of the USENET (short for *users' network*) service furnished by the

Internet. Information intended for a particular type of audience can be assigned by the author to an electronic "bulletin board."

A single message posted on a popular bulletin board or sent to a mailing list might reach and engage millions of people. . . . Each bulletin board or newsgroup has a name, and anyone interested can "hang out" there. . . . Almost any topic you can name has a group communicating about it on the network. (Gates, 1995, pp. 123-125)

A second publishing option involves authors creating their own websites and placing a report of their research on those sites. Potential readers can find the report by entering key words into a search engine (such engines as Google, Altavista, Ask Jeeves, or Teoma)—that is, key words relating to the teacher's topic. An important advantage of placing a report on one's own website is that there are no restrictions on the length of the report.

A third way to publish on the Internet is to transmit the manuscript via the Internet to the editor of a journal or magazine that issues its products on the World Wide Web, such as *Health Education Research, Journal of Deaf Studies and Deaf Education, Applied Linguistics,* and *Contemporary Issues in Early Childhood.* With the costs of print publishing rising and the number of subscribers to many scholarly journals declining, traditional journals have suffered serious financial difficulties. Thus, a growing number are turning to electronic publishing. University libraries can usually furnish an author the names of electronic periodicals suitable for publishing the kind of report the author has prepared.

Publishing via e-mail or one's own website has a number of advantages over print media. First, e-mail or a website delivers the finished product to readers far earlier than does print publishing. With printed journals and books, a year or two can elapse between the time a completed manuscript is submitted to editors and the time that the work is finally available to the public. With electronic publishing, there is little or no wait between when the author puts the report on the network and when it becomes available to readers. Furthermore, electronic publishing eliminates problems of distance. Internet users anywhere on Earth can receive the researcher's publication as soon as it appears. Whereas traditional journals and books cannot conveniently be altered once they are in print, materials on the web can be revised at any time—corrected, lengthened, updated. Publishing over the network also enables the author to receive rapid feedback from readers who send their comments to the author by e-mail. Documents placed on the Internet can include full-color illustrations to accompany the text, which is an expensive feature in print media but is included at little cost on the Internet. Finally, e-mail or website publishing permits the author to maintain complete control over the form and content of the report, because no editors are involved, except in the case of formal Internet journals and books that must pass through the editorial process before they are issued on the Internet. However, a disadvantage of shortcutting the editorial process is that the author then lacks the professional aid with the writing style and the elimination of errors that editors usually provide.

Books and Book Chapters

Occasionally a teacher's research will be of sufficient size and importance to warrant its publication in book form. Often such research has been conducted for a doctoral dissertation. In that case, the book will usually not be an exact reproduction of the dissertation but, rather, will be a revised manuscript more suitable for the intended reading audience.

One way to find the names of publishers that might be interested in the teacher's manuscript is by browsing in a well-stocked library to locate books bearing on the topics treated in the manuscript. The publishers of such volumes usually maintain Internet websites that offer potential authors detailed information about the sorts of books their companies issue and about how to submit manuscripts for editors' consideration. When an author first corresponds with a publisher via the regular mail or e-mail, the editors usually do not want to receive an entire manuscript. Instead, they prefer an outline of chapter contents, an estimate of the likely reading audience, a description of the contribution that the book would make to such readers, and two or three sample chapters that illustrate the author's writing style.

An advantage of a book over such media as oral presentations and articles in periodicals is that the book not only allows an author to report the study in detail, but it also provides more space in which to describe the theoretical foundations and practical applications of the research.

Rather than issue their work as an entire book, teachers far more often will contribute a single chapter to a volume that is composed of chapters by different authors. The opportunity to have one's work included in such an edited collection usually appears in one of three ways.

First, a person who is editing a volume focusing on a particular topic selects chapter authors who are known to be experts on the topic. Editors locate such contributors by noting who has written authoritative journal articles and books in the field of interest and by asking colleagues to suggest the names of potential authors.

Second, an editor selects a variety of already-published journal articles or excerpts from books and reissues them as chapters of the editor's own volume.

Third, papers presented at a conference can comprise a book's contents. Examples of volumes published from selected papers at three conferences of the Comparative and International Education Society's western region are *Human Rights and Education*—13 chapters (Tarrow, 1987), *Education's Role in National Development Plans*—12 chapters (Thomas, 1992), and *Education in the Urban Context*—12 chapters (Stromquist, 1994).

Editors of collections can vary considerably in the amount of control they seek to exert over the form, content, and quality of contributors' chapters. Some editors publish the offerings without change, except for correcting spelling and grammar errors. Others return manuscripts to authors with directions for substantial changes, or the editor may even choose to rewrite a manuscript. Because the quality of chapters submitted for an edited volume often varies considerably from one author to another, an editor may accept certain manuscripts in their initial form but revise others in minor or major ways.

Planning Guide

To practice preparing a research report for publication in a journal or bulletin, try the following activity.

1. *Project focus.* Identify the research project you wish to publish. That project may be one you have already completed or one that you are in the process of conducting. Or you can simply imagine a study that you might carry out.

2. *Key terms.* Find key words in the title or contents of your project that relate to the subject-matter or focus of the research.

3. *Appropriate journals.* Use the key words as your guides in locating journals for which your report would be suitable. Your hunt for relevant periodicals can involve searching both the Internet and libraries' journal holdings. (For help in conducting the Internet search, you may wish to consult Chapter 3 earlier in this book. Lists of journals are easily located by entering such terms as *academic journals* or *professional journals* into a search engine.)

4. *Website information.* From a journal's website, copy information concerning (a) types of articles accepted, (b) appropriate length of articles, (c) format requirements, (d) the number of copies of articles to be submitted, and (e) where to submit manuscripts.

5. *Journal analysis.* From inspecting one or more issues of a journal found in a library or in someone's personal collection, answer the following questions:

5.1 In terms of the number of printed pages, what is the length of the shortest article and the length of the longest article in the journal? What is the typical number of words per page? Now convert length-in-pages to length-in-words by multiplying the longest and shortest articles' page-lengths by the average number of words per page to arrive at how many words you could include in a manuscript intended for that journal.

5.2 Is each article preceded by an abstract of the article's contents? If so, how many words are in a typical abstract?

5.3 Is the article divided into sections? If so, are the section titles in one article the same as in the rest of the articles, or are authors allowed to decide what the titles of sections will be?

5.4 Within the body of articles, what is the style for citing references to sources of information?

5.5 Are references cast as footnotes at the bottom of pages or is there a list of references (bibliography) at the end of the article?

5.6 In articles' references or bibliographies, what components are included, in what style, and in what order? (The word *components* refers to authors' names, article or book title, publication date, and name and location of the publisher.)

6. Finally, write a summary of the information you compiled in steps 1 through 5 above.

References

Allen, J. D. (1982). Classroom management: Students' goals, perspectives, and strategies. *American Educational Research Journal, 23* (3), 437-459.

Burkett, E. (2001). *Another planet—A year in the life of a suburban high school.* New York: HarperCollins.

Denzin, N. K. (1989, 1997). *Interpretive ethnography.* Thousand Oaks: Sage.

Dissertation Abstracts Online. (2003). http://wwwlibrary. dialog.com/ bluesheets/html/bl0035.html.

Gates, B. (1995). *The road ahead.* New York: Viking.

Glass, G. V., McGaw, B., & Smith, M. L. (1981). *Meta-analysis in social research.* Thousand Oaks, CA: Sage.

Hunter, J. E., Schmidt, F. L., & Jackson, G. B. (1982). *Meta-analysis: Cumulating research findings across studies.* Beverly Hills, CA: Sage.

Internet users will top 1 billion in 2005. (2002, March 21). *Computer industry alamanc* (press release). Online. Available: http://www.c-I-a. com/pr032102.html.

McGaw, B. (1985). Meta-analysis. In T. Husén & T. N. Postlethwaite (Eds.), *International encyclopedia of education: Research and studies* (1st ed., vol. 6, pp. 3322-3330). Oxford: Pergamon.

Postlethwaite, T. N., & Ross, K. N. (1992). *Effective schools in reading.* The Hague, Netherlands: The International Association for the Evaluation of Educational Achievement.

Ross, K. N. (1985). Sampling. In T. Husén & T. N. Postlethwaite (Eds.). *International encyclopedia of education: Research and studies* (1st ed., vol. 8, pp. 4370-4381). Oxford: Pergamon.

Stossel, S. (2001, November 28). Back to school. *Atlantic Unbound.* Online. Available: http://www.theatlantic.com/unbound/interviews/int 2001-11-28.htm.

Stromquist, N. (Ed.). (1994). *Education in the urban context.* Westport, CT: Praeger.

Tarrow, N. B. (Ed.). (1987). *Human rights and education.* Oxford: Pergamon.

Thomas, R. M. (Ed.). (1992). *Education's role in national development plans.* Westport, CT: Praeger.

Thomas, R. M. (1998). *Conducting educational research.* Westport, CT: Bergin & Garvey.

Thomas, R. M., & Murray, P. V. (1982). *CASES—A resource guide for teaching about the law.* Glenview, IL: Scott, Foresman.

White, L. A. (1994). The concept of culture. In *Encyclopaedia Britannica,* Vol. 16, pp. 874-878. Chicago: Encyclopaedia Britannica.

Wolcott, H. F. (1988). Ethnographic research in education. In R. M. Jaeger (Ed.), *Complementary methods of research in education* (pp. 187-210). Washington, DC: American Educational Research Association.

Index